Best Water Plants

Stefan Buczacki
Best Water Plants

HAMLYN

Executive Art Editor Mark Richardson
Designer Michael Whitehead
Editor Selina Higgins
Production Melanie Frantz
Picture Research Jenny Faithfull

First published in Great Britain in 1995
by Hamlyn an imprint of Reed Consumer Books Limited
Michelin House, 81 Fulham Road, London SW3 6RB
and Auckland, Melbourne, Singapore and Toronto

Produced by Imprimerie Pollina SA - n° 66773
Printed in France

ISBN 0 600 58337 6

A catalogue of this book is available at the British Library

CONTENTS

INTRODUCTION 6
  Water as a Garden Feature 8
  Creating a Water Garden 10
  Types of Water Garden Plant 14
  Planting, Feeding and Aftercare 16
  Propagation 17
  Other Pool Life 18
  Problems 20

PLANT DIRECTORY
  Marginals 22
  Water Plants 38
  Submerged Plants 52
  Floating Plants 60
  Bog Plants 66
  Ferns 102
  Grasses 106
  Bog Garden Trees and Shrubs 118

Index 124
Photograph Acknowledgements 127
Temperature Chart 127

INTRODUCTION

I can't think how long it is since I gardened without some form of water feature, and now I couldn't imagine going into my garden without hearing the familiar sound of moving water. This book is about gardening with water, the range of features of which water is an essential part, the way such features can be incorporated into the rest of the garden, the way in which they can be constructed, and above all, the range of plants that can be grown in and around the water. It is in this last area that I feel gardeners have been least well served and that the average garden centre has some catching up to do.

A wide variety of plants can be grown beside a slow-moving stream

While the range of water garden appliances, equipment and aids has never been greater, and the technology never simpler or less expensive, these developments don't seem to have been matched by any increased availability of the numerous beautiful types of water plant. Go into the average retail gardening outlet and you will find perhaps three or four water lily varieties, half a dozen other water plants, a dozen marginals and not a great deal more. Little attention is given to plants tolerant of (let alone requiring) the wet soil that is so crucial to establishing a bog garden. No-one of course, can force retailers to extend their range but I hope that the ever-increasing interest in water gardening and the knowledge that a very large number of desirable plants exists will encourage more gardeners to ask for them.

On pp.10-13, I have provided precise information on how to create your own water garden and the pitfalls of which you should be aware. I hope, however, that one message above all will come across: water gardening is one of the most rewarding of all types of garden cultivation. The remainder of the book is subdivided according to plant groups, based largely on the type of water garden habitat that they require. It is worth noting that many water plants are vigorous and invasive and for this reason the choice of species and varieties, especially if you

have only a small pool, is very important. In several sections of the book, therefore, I have made reference to pool size in my recommendations and while I don't wish this to be interpreted as a rigid rule, I have in mind the following approximate pool sizes in each category: small pools, up to 1.75 x 1.25m (5½ x 4ft) with a maximum depth of about 30cm (12in); medium pools, up to 3 x 1.75m (10 x 5½ft) with a depth of about 45cm (18in); large pools, at least 4.25 x 3m (14 x 10ft) with a maximum depth of at least 60cm (24in).

Water lilies can be combined with pretty marginals in a larger pond

WATER AS A GARDEN FEATURE

Once gardeners have had a water feature in the garden, I don't believe they will ever garden without one again. Even in gardens frequented by small children, where the feature should be one that excludes an open pool area, the old adage holds true: water does bring any garden to life. And although the term 'water garden' for many people conjures up an image simply of a pool, in reality the subject matter is much wider. Not only will water gardens, by the sight and sound of water, influence the appearance and feel of the garden as a whole, but the type of water feature should, itself, be dictated by the overall style of the garden.

Water lilies can be used to break the surface of a formal sunken pool

I'll begin with garden pools, which fall into two main types: the formal and the informal. The formal pool has hard edges of stone, brick or slabs that create a more or less angular boundary in a paved courtyard, terrace, patio or similar area. There is no doubt where the pool ends and the surrounding area begins, and the whole is unashamedly artificial but none the worse for that. The largest, finest and most spectacular water gardens in the world are all quite formal creations. Notable examples include the fountains of the Villa d'Este near Rome, those at the palace of Versailles, the Alhambra in Granada and the cascade at Chatsworth, central England. But in such a pool, there will be only limited scope for planting marginal plants on ledges just below the water surface. The remainder of the planting around the pool must, of necessity, be of plants in containers but these, of course, will not be water garden species. Formal pools are often enhanced by some form of fountain and perhaps a sculpture or ornamental fountain-head too.

The alternative form of pool, the informal or semi-natural, is more versatile for it merges softly at the edges with other plantings – marginal areas, bog gardens that themselves vary from very wet to drier parts, normal garden beds and borders, shrubberies or, very effectively, rock gardens. The edges of the pool are irregular and such water movement as there is will be more appropriately provided by waterfalls than by fountains, while in very large gardens, very large semi-natural pools blend imperceptibly with lakes.

At the other extreme in pool size is the tub garden, suitable for those with very limited space who hanker for a real pool. I confess that my own preference for a water feature in a small area is some form of self-contained re-circulating fountain, for this can combine the appealing trickling sound with the absence of open water that is so dangerous if small children are

A small waterfall in a natural stream creates movement in the garden

around. It is also perfectly possible to create a small-scale, modern version of a classical wall fountain, with an ornamental spout from which water cascades into some form of collecting trough, before draining away to a concealed tank.

For many gardeners, the ultimate water garden has a stream running through it but unless you are blessed with a natural watercourse, my advice is not to try to create one. Although modern recirculating pumps make the water flow technically possible, I have yet to see an artificial stream that looks right. I don't doubt they can be

created but they do need very great skill and entail considerable expense. If, however, you are fortunate enough to have a natural stream, do ensure that your plans comply with any local water authority regulations before you begin to plant up the banks and certainly before you attempt any constructions that would affect the flow of the water. Although you may own the land over which the stream flows, you will not own the water in it, nor have the rights to change anything (or even, very probably, be allowed to fish in it). Once you have satisfied yourself that you are on the correct side of the

regulations, bear in mind that most pool plants will not thrive in running water, and that any plants on the stream banks will probably have to survive being immersed for much of the winter, and dried out for much of the summer. You would be well advised to look at native species that grow naturally in such conditions and concentrate on them.

The siting of a water feature in a garden is not simply a matter of selecting a spot in which it will look right, for all pools, of whatever type, have certain requirements in common. First and foremost, they must have the maximum exposure to sunlight. Water plants and most marginals will not thrive in shade, while the pool itself will suffer if leaves drop into it from deciduous trees and decompose in the water. The routine scooping out of fallen leaves with a net in the autumn will be essential in any event for they blow considerable distances and seem magnetically attracted to open water. Bog gardens may, however, be placed quite effectively in partial shade at least and many of the bog garden plants that I recommend are shade tolerant. Further information on shade tolerant plants can be obtained from Book 3 of this series, *Best Shade Plants*.

It may seem self-evident, but pools must be positioned on level ground if they are not to overflow. Level ground at the foot of a slope is ideal if you also plan to have a bog garden, for moisture will constantly be replenished by rainwater draining downhill. A pool alone at the foot of a slope, however, will create problems as it will almost constantly flood in winter.

CREATING A WATER GARDEN

Water gardens of all types are immeasurably easier and cheaper to create today than ever before. The use of puddled clay and, later, concrete to line pools has almost entirely given way to various types of plastic, either in preformed shapes or in versatile flexible sheet. Preformed pool liners, rather like large babies' bathtubs provide the cheapest and quickest way of creating a pool but they have limitations: they are suitable only for small or fairly small pools; they offer you no opportunity to use your imagination or initiative to select your own pool shape; some are still manufactured in wholly inappropriate bright colours (swimming pool blue seems to be a favourite); you will be limited by the position of the ledges for the positioning of your plants; they are seldom deep enough to give fish a sanctuary from freezing conditions in winter and they are extremely difficult to disguise. In short, a preformed liner, no matter how long it is in place and how carefully it is planted, will, to my mind, always look like a preformed liner. If you decide that this is the best option for you, however, do be sure to choose a liner made from glass fibre and/or one with a guaranteed life-span of at least 15 years.

It will be evident from my comments above that I very strongly favour the use of flexible sheet but it is most important to buy the type sold specially for pool use. Normal polythene sheet, no matter how thick, is simply not good enough. It doesn't have the correct flexibility and stretching properties, and it will readily puncture and tear. Polyvinyl chloride (PVC) is much better, more durable, should be guaranteed for at least 10 years and is relatively cheap. Best of all, but also most expensive, is butyl rubber, a synthetic, flexible rubber-like material which is normally guaranteed for around 20 years but should last considerably longer.

BUILDING A POOL WITH A PREFORMED LINER

Having given careful consideration to the siting factors that I outlined on p.9, lay your pool liner on the ground and mark out the shape with pegs or with a flexible hosepipe, allowing about 25-30cm (10-12in) more area all round than the size of the liner itself. Dig out a hole to the depth of the liner, plus about 5-7cm (2-3in), taking account of any ledges or ridges within the liner. Lay sand in the bottom of the hole to

a depth of about 5-7cm (2-3in) (to take up the additional depth) and carefully place the liner on to the sand such that the lip of the liner is flush with the surrounding soil surface. Check carefully at this stage that the soil surface is level all around the edges of the pool; otherwise you will forever have the frustration of a pool with a greater depth to the water surface at one end than the other. Then pour in sand to fill in the gap between the sides of the liner and the sides of the hole.

The next step is to provide some form of edging to the pool to prevent the surrounding soil from falling in. This can be done either with regular stone slabs thus creating a formal pool or irregularly arranged ones for a

Remember to mark out the perimeters of a pool before starting to dig

Use a spirit level to ensure the sides of the new water garden are level

will be stood, and make a shallow shelf, approximately 20cm (8in) wide, all around the edge for marginal plants. Lay the flexible sheet across the hole, temporarily anchoring it with rocks, and then slowly begin to pour water from a hosepipe into the centre. The liner will gradually stretch to fill the contours of the pool so you will need to move the anchoring rocks to accommodate this. Once the pool is almost full, trim the liner to give an overlap of about 20cm (8in) all round the edge and set slabs or bricks on this in the usual way for a formal pool, or more irregular rocks for an informal one. Fill in any gaps between the rocks with soil to create an area that can be very attractively planted alongside an informal pool and a bog garden. Creeping plants will soon grow over and disguise the boundary wall.

BUILDING A BOG GARDEN

A bog garden requires an area of permanently wet soil and may be constructed in a similar way to a pool using a flexible liner. The ideal depth is about 45cm (18in) and, as before, the liner should be bedded on sand, but it should also have a number of holes punched in it because, although the bog garden is permanently wet, it should have through drainage. An area with no through drainage will become waterlogged and anaerobic decomposition will take place, leading to foul conditions. Fill the bog garden with good garden soil, ideally mixed with well-rotted garden compost and coarse grit in the ratio by volume of 3:2:1. I always prefer to mound the soil in the centre in order to create a gradient of moisture content in the soil and so allow the growing of a wide

semi-natural planting but, in both cases, it is important to use mortar to provide a rigid and secure boundary. If you are fortunate and the liner has trough type ledges within, these may be filled with soil for planting. If, as usual, they are simply shelves, it will be necessary to have all of your plants secured in baskets first.

BUILDING A POOL WITH A FLEXIBLE LINER

Mark out the shape of your pool on the ground, and as ever you will find that using a hosepipe is the easiest

way to 'draw' curves. Then measure a rectangle that will accommodate the size and shape you have drawn and add approximately 60cm (24in) in width and length to give the actual size of sheet that you require. The additions are to allow for the depth of the pool, which at its deepest part should be at least 45cm (18in), and to give an overlap at the sides over which rocks, slabs and soil will be laid.

Dig the hole for the pool, making sure that you create ledges of different depths on which planting baskets

CREATING A WATER GARDEN

range of bog garden plants. It is important not to allow the bog garden to dry out in summer, and positioning it at a natural low point in the garden will help with this. Another way to maintain the moisture content of a bog garden is to channel water from the rainwater drainpipe of a greenhouse or outbuilding through a plastic pipe below soil level.

RAISED POOLS

The idea of creating a raised pool may seem as logical as requiring a downhill lake for water-skiing. But think of it simply as a raised bed filled with water instead of soil and it will make sense. The basic construction method is the same as for a conventional pool, the stone or brick retaining wall taking over the function of the hole, and

lined with a liner bedded on sand. Raised pools can look very attractive in formal courtyard plantings; some of the most effective are circular and one of the best that I know is at the lovely and famous gardens of Hidcote Manor in Gloucestershire, England. They are also very much appreciated by disabled gardeners who can easily draw alongside in a wheelchair.

WATER MOVEMENT
AND WATER LIGHTING

As I have, I hope, already conveyed, a water garden really comes into its own if there is some water movement, like a fountain in a formal pool, or a waterfall in an informal one. There are no rules about the type of fountain you should have and the choice of a single jet, a multiple spray

head or some other device is a personal one. Almost all possibilities can be achieved with a modern, low-voltage submersible pump with watertight seals and magnetic couplings. The pump remains permanently immersed and is connected to the mains via low-voltage wire, run from a transformer at the nearest indoor socket to avoid the normal danger from mixing water and electricity. I have used such a pump very effectively by adapting the outlet to enable it to be attached to an antique lead fountain-head spout, and similar options are open to anyone with a modicum of DIY knowledge. My only word of caution with fountains is to advise you not to have too much of a water spray, as this can have an excessive cooling effect on the

A flexible liner filled with garden soil forms the base for a bog garden

pool, to the overall detriment of plants and fish; I would also advise that, as far as possible, fountains shouldn't cascade permanently on to water lily foliage, which seems to resent too much spray.

Waterfalls are also easily created using modern pumps, either submersible or non-submersible models and, once again, unless the feature is to be very large and the necessary pumping back is to take place against a considerable gradient, low voltage, DIY pumps will be perfectly adequate. Pump manufacturers almost always give full instructions on the use of pumps to create waterfalls.

Pool lighting is very much a matter of taste. Once again, the modern low voltage systems are inexpensively and easily laid, and while I can usually sympathize with spotlights used close to a pool to highlight plant life, I am much less certain about the coloured, submerged lighting which always seems to create an effect more in keeping with a night club than a garden feature. But, as I say, it is a matter of taste and if that is your taste, then you must have as you please.

Stone slabs can be used as a border to edge a pool

TYPES OF WATER GARDEN PLANT

All plants, even desert species, require moisture in order to grow but my interest in this book is in those that require rather more than an average amount of water in the environment. There is a range of species that can be most usefully grouped according to how wet are the conditions that they prefer.

At the greatest extreme are the **submerged plants** that live entirely or almost entirely submerged, sometimes hardly even rooted in the pool mud and emerging above the water surface, if at all, only to flower. They might be thought scarcely worthy of cultivation but, in reality, are among the most important pool plants because oxygen diffuses from their leaves into the water and thus they benefit other plants, fish and other forms of water life. Nonetheless, in saying this, I am merely repeating conventional wisdom for I have found that it is on and around the submerged plants that much troublesome blanket weed develops (see p.20), and I have had very successful garden pools that contained no oxygenating plants at all and in which the oxygenating role was completely taken over by the pool fountain.

Floating plants are those that, believe it or not, simply float. Some have no roots, some have roots that dangle into the water, but none are anchored in any way. They die down in the winter to survive as dormant buds, resting in the mud of the pool floor to grow and rise again with the arrival of warmer conditions in the spring. Many species of floating plant multiply vegetatively with great rapidity and, in consequence, can cause serious problems if they are allowed into rivers, canals or other water courses, as they can cause severe blockages. For this reason, their sale may be restricted in some warmer climates where the winter offers less of a check to their development.

The group that I have called simply **water plants** are those that grow within the pool, anchored in the mud but with leaves and flowers arising to float at the surface or to rise above it. Water lilies are the classic water plants and they exemplify one of the most important features of the group, in that the depth of water to which they are most suited and the vigour of their surface spread varies considerably between varieties which must, therefore, be chosen carefully.

Plants that grow at the very edge of the water are called **marginals**. The group covers a wide range of habitat requirements, from those species that must exist permanently in several centimetres of water through those that tolerate periodic drying out of the water's edge, to those that need saturated, waterlogged soil but not actually standing water. The marginals will grade almost imperceptibly into the plants of the **bog garden** which

A pool featuring a good collection of floating plants

comprise the largest section of the book. The bog garden is the most varied habitat, for at one extreme are the plants that are only one step removed from the marginals that need very wet soil, while at the other end there are those species that require moisture-retentive soil but which are intolerant of any waterlogging. A number of them would be described simply as border perennials but I have included them here for I believe that the more informal type of water garden, which often includes a bog garden, should grade gradually into the other, drier parts of the garden. In the bog garden section (pp.66-101) therefore, I have given an indication (high, moderate or low soil moisture) as to which part of the bog garden is most appropriate for each of the species.

A well-filled garden can contain a wide range of different water-loving plants

PLANTING, FEEDING AND AFTERCARE

By and large, water plants require rather less routine care and attention than almost any other type of garden plant. With one or two possible exceptions among some barely hardy, floating forms, none of them are grown as annuals so there is no routine raising and renewal of plants to consider. I have given notes on propagation for each species because it may be necessary, from time to time, to increase or renew your stock but it is never an annual chore. Indeed, as I mentioned earlier, in a number of cases, limiting propagation is more the order of the day for, as a group, water plants include a disproportionate number of vigorous forms.

Decorative water plants grown in baskets add variety and colour

For the various groups that actually grow within the water of the pool, planting is simplicity itself: for most submerged and floating plants, the operation comprises merely dropping them into the water. Attaching a small weight to a clump of shoots may be necessary for those submerged types that are to take root in the mud at the pool bottom. Water plants and marginals may be planted directly into the mud or into planting baskets containing soil, which are lowered or placed into the chosen spot. Once handmade of wicker, these baskets are now manufactured in moulded plastic and are sold in various sizes, appropriate for different sizes of plant. Planting into a basket overcomes the difficulty (and sometimes danger) of trying to plant into the deep water of an established pool but it also has the advantages of allowing plants to be lifted for periodic division or renewal and, most importantly, of limiting the spread of particularly invasive marginal species when grown in restricted spaces. When planting baskets are to be placed within the pool, it is important to place a layer of about 3cm (1½in) of clean grit over the soil surface and around the crown of the plant otherwise fish will disturb the soil and easily uproot the plants from their settled positions.

Whether the plants are planted into baskets, directly into ledges within the pool or at the pool edge, it is essential to use soil to which no organic matter or fertilizer has been added, as this will both foul the water and encourage the growth of blanket weed and other algae. Soil from a relatively neglected part of the garden is ideal. Feeding water garden plants is simple; purpose-made sachets of specially formulated fertilizer are available for placing beneath the water plants at planting time, but I have never used these and have never found them necessary. The only water garden plants that I do feed are those in the bog garden which I feed in exactly the same way as, but to a rather lesser degree than border perennials, giving a light dressing of general fertilizer, such as fish blood and bone in the spring. I also mulch them in autumn and spring, for even bog gardens can become drier during the summer, and it is the spring mulch which is intended to keep the roots fully moist, while the autumn mulch will offer protection from any penetrating winter frosts. Whenever possible, however, I do use composts rather than animal manures when mulching bog garden plants.

There are few water-garden perennials that require staking and notes on any cutting back or pruning necessary are given under the individual descriptions. But I must repeat that, by and large, water garden plants are little trouble.

PROPAGATION

Almost without exception, the water plants in this book are perennials. But as I often find myself having to explain, perennial does not equate with immortal and so, at times, you will need to replenish your stock. And I say replenish rather than replace for even an old and overgrown plant can often be rescued by knowing how it is best propagated. Whichever method you select, you will almost certainly find yourself with more plants than you need but you can share them with friends. I find that this is something especially appreciated with water plants since nurseries and garden centres tend to restrict themselves to a limited range of species and varieties. If you have something unusual, what better way for it to become better known than for you to propagate and distribute it?

DIVISION

The simplest method of propagation, and the one applicable to most types of water plant is by division – the splitting of an existing plant into several smaller parts. Apart from some of the hardier bog garden species, much the best time to divide is in the spring, as the air, soil and water are beginning to warm up but before growth has really started. Dig up the plant, or lift it if it is in a planting basket. The old basket should be cut away and disposed of and the clump split by whatever means is appropriate. Discard the old, congested parts of the plant from the centre and only replant the small, vigorous pieces from the periphery.

CUTTINGS

I find only two types of cutting are of value in the propagation of water plants: stem cuttings (those that with normal terrestrial plants would be called softwood or semi-ripe cuttings) and, sometimes, leaf-bud cuttings. Hormone rooting powder may be used with all of them.

All cuttings should be rooted in either a propagator or a covered cold-frame. It is very important to maintain a moist atmosphere around all cuttings. Use a hand sprayer to mist over the cuttings regularly. The effectiveness of the type of medium into which the cuttings are placed varies from one type of plant to another and I have given my suggestions in the individual descriptions.

Stem cuttings should be about 15cm (6in) long, be removed from the parent plant with a clean cut made just below a bud and the large leaves trimmed off. They should be inserted to a depth of approximately 5cm (2in) in the rooting medium. Leaf-bud cuttings should comprise a leaf with adjoining bud and about 1cm (½in) of stem either side. They should be inserted so that the bud is below the surface of the rooting medium.

SEED

Many types of water plant *can* be raised from seed although it has to be said that many perennial forms are selected varieties that give rise to rather variable offspring when multiplied in this way and are indeed better propagated by cuttings, or bought as named plants. I have indicated in the text where this is so. The few annual species of course must be raised from seed and this can be done either directly outdoors ('the hardy annual technique') or into a seedling compost under protection (the 'half-hardy annual technique'), the seedling then being hardened-off before planting out.

Sowing seeds and raising seedlings on the greenhouse bench or even on the kitchen window ledge is not only easy, it is also very satisfying. You will require a compost in which to sow the seed, a propagator in which to put the compost, water, in most instances light and a means of supplying an adequate temperature. The compost should be at least based on a proprietary mixture, either soil-based or soilless but often with the addition of some sand. Always use fresh compost for each batch of seeds.

Generally, seeds require a slightly higher temperature in order to germinate than the plants ever require again. Moreover, within fairly well defined limits for each type of seed, the higher the temperature the more rapid and uniform the germination. Provision of an adequate and appropriate temperature is thus very important and as the seed of some water plants can be somewhat stubborn in germinating, it is worth giving a little attention to providing the correct temperature. Once germinated and hardened-off, grow on perennial species in pots, which must be kept constantly moist, feeding them in the meantime, and then planted out, in the following year.

OTHER POOL LIFE

Water gardens are special among garden features in that much of their appeal arises from the various living things that are found there, whether naturally occurring, or introduced. They are also unusual in that our introductions aren't limited to plants for, in order to achieve the necessary balance within the pool, animals are required too. Pool animals primarily, of course, consist of fish but they should be selected carefully. You must not only choose the types of fish that are most appropriate and compatible with your pool but also ensure that they are of the correct size and quantity.

Fish and water lilies together create the traditional image of a pond

Serious fish keepers will refer to specialist literature and, if they aspire to such choice specimens as Koi carp, will want to create pools and conditions specifically for them. For the normal garden pool, however, Koi are inappropriate as they will uproot plants and create general mayhem, and will require protection from herons and, indeed, potential thieves, for fine specimens are very valuable indeed. I have, in fact, now come to the conclusion that because of the threat from herons which exists in almost all parts of the British Isles, investing in any expensive and precious fish simply isn't worthwhile for an ornamental domestic garden pool. All methods of protection, be it by netting, alarms or scaring devices, are necessarily unsightly and I prefer to take the chance with less valuable fish.

The best inexpensive ornamental fish to choose are goldfish and their multi-coloured relatives, shubunkins, with the longer-tailed comet forms probably the prettiest of all. I like to combine them with a number of the more slender golden orfe and a few golden rudd. I have never found it necessary to have bottom-dwelling fish such as loach or tench which remain permanently out of sight and don't in reality have any special merit as scavengers. Of other fish that you are likely to see on offer, carp are too large and are too damaging to plant life while minnows are only really successful in larger pools with constantly moving water; they are river not still-water fish. In larger pools, sticklebacks may be successful although they can feel threatened and be aggressive to other, much larger fish.

My advice is to buy fish of approximately 10cm (4in) or more in length. I find that if they are much smaller or very much larger than this, a number of losses is to be expected when they are first introduced into the pool.

Ponds will attract all manner of amphibian life

resulting shock waves can kill the fish.

A pool is the only part of the garden in which snails are welcome, for the aquatic species are not damaging to plant life in the same way as their terrestrial relatives. They have some value as scavengers in feeding on dead plant material but contrary to what is sometimes suggested, they won't help in controlling algal growth and 'green' water. Although you may buy water snails of various types from specialist water garden suppliers, they will inevitably be introduced on water plants and, indeed, as eggs adhering to birds' feet. It is often said that the common pond snail is more damaging to water plants than the rather more attractive flat-shelled ramshorn snail but I have never found this so and, in reality, the ramshorn seems less well adapted to pool life than its common cousin and may die out in time.

There is no need to introduce any other water creatures but, as I have already indicated, many more will arrive of their own accord. There seems to be nothing you can do to ensure that frogs and newts will find your pool appealing but if they do happen to come along, they should be welcomed. In large pools and lakes, ducks and other water fowl will be attracted, while dragonflies and damselflies are the most spectacular of the insects that you will see, although countless others will appear both in and above the water. From time to time, gardeners express concern about small wriggling creatures that they see in the water of their pools. I can but assure them that many things in pools wriggle but none need cause them any concern.

Numbers of fish are only likely to be critical in a small pool when between 12 and 20 will be about right. Fish shouldn't be introduced into a pool until about three weeks after the plants have had a chance to settle down and, at first, they will disappear to the deeper water for two or more weeks. Once they begin to appear at the surface, however, they should be fed, most easily with proprietary floating fish food as frequently as the manufacturers advise.

During the winter, part of the pool surface must be kept free of ice in order for gas exchange to take place, without which the fish will die. The most effective way is with a small, low-voltage floating heater, or simply by keeping the fountain running continuously, but carefully pouring hot water into one corner will also do the job. I find that floating objects designed to keep the surface moving are rarely satisfactory but, certainly, the ice should never be smashed as the

PROBLEMS

Yet another advantage offered by water plants is that they are relatively free from pest and disease problems; and, I might add somewhat cynically, a further benefit is that rather little can be done about those problems that do occur. This is because fungicidal and insecticidal sprays must not be used on any water garden plant (with the possible exception of bog garden species positioned well away from the water) for the simple reason that most have adverse effects on other pool inhabitants. Derris, for instance, that natural plant product widely used as a general insecticide and much vaunted as a 'safe' product by the organic gardening fraternity, is notoriously toxic to all fish.

Aphids are the commonest pests in water gardens and are most readily disposed of by being washed off with a hosepipe; then they will fall into the water and be generally appreciated by fish as an additional source of protein. Fungal leaf spots are the commonest disease problem and seriously affected leaves should be cut off and disposed of. Mildew can be troublesome on some marginal and water garden plants but it tends not to be serious until temperatures rise during the summer and, provided this takes place after flowering, the plants can be at least partially cut back and the badly affected foliage taken away.

It is so often the case in gardening that the plants that have been most intensively bred and selected tend to be those on which pest and disease problems are the most severe; think of carnations, dahlias, potatoes and chrysanthemums . The water garden equivalent is the water lily, which is affected by a wider range of pests and diseases than any other, but rather few are generally serious. The exception is, perhaps, the water lily beetle, a small brown beetle with small brown larvae, both of which eat out holes and furrows in the upper surface of the leaves, not only causing disfigurement, but more importantly, allowing fungal decay to set in. For the reasons given here, insecticidal control cannot be used and, once again, treatment comprises a combination of the hosepipe to wash off the insects and vigilance so that prompt action can be taken at the first sign of symptoms appearing.

Without doubt, the biggest problems in garden pools relate not to pests or diseases on individual plants but to the pool water itself. Over the years, I have received more questions about the prevention and/or elimination of green 'slime' and of green 'pea-soup' water than any other water garden subject. Both problems are algal in origin, for green slime is a growth of filamentous green alga, commonly called blanket weed, while the pea-soup appearance of garden pool water results from the build up of vast populations of microscopic, single-celled green algae in a process sometimes called 'blooming'. Over many years of water gardening, I have come firmly to the conclusion that neither can be prevented once present, and neither can totally or predictably be eliminated but, conversely, I don't think either are nearly as serious as is sometimes claimed.

Water lilies can suffer from severe aphid infection

I have said elsewhere in this book that I believe that submerged oxygenating plants (and especially *Elodea*) encourage blanket weed by providing it with a base on which to grow; and that I have had successful pools without oxygenators and without blanket weed. But if you do grow submerged plants, as you must if there is no other means of providing oxygen, be doubly careful in checking all new plant introductions. You cannot always see filaments of blanket weed adhering to them but, if you do, then reject them. I have been told several times that filling a pool with rainwater rather than tap water will significantly lessen algal growth and this makes sense, for it will contain less of the chemicals that can be used by the algae as a nitrogen source. It must be admitted that filling your pool with rainwater every time is easier said than done. But whatever type of water you use, it is important to prevent any run-off of fertilizer from adjacent parts of the garden. One particularly common source of this is containers of plants standing near to the pool's edge. When these are given liquid fertilizer, run-off into the pool can very easily occur and, as a general rule, pots should be temporarily moved away from the water when applying feed.

Once blanket weed is established in a pool, I don't believe that adding proprietary algicidal chemicals to the water is the correct solution. They may well kill the algae and may even do so without directly harming other life in the pool, but the result will be dead blanket weed which will decompose in the water and so create an even worse state of affairs. Physical

removal of blanket weed is, without doubt, the best method of control. By physical removal, I mean rolling up your sleeves and pulling it out if the pool is small enough to be reached; alternatively, twist the weed around a wooden forked stick (not a metal tool if the pool has a plastic liner) and pull it out. If practicable, it's always sensible to dump the blanket weed into an old tub or similar container to allow small fish and newts to escape before it is composted.

I am frequently asked about the use of filters for garden pools, as two basic types, mechanical and biological, are now widely advertised. I have used both on an experimental basis and have misgivings about their value; I do not use either routinely. The principle of the mechanical filter is that the water is pumped continuously through some form of filter pad which removes suspended particles, including the green algae. They are small,

submersed, fairly unobtrusive and the same pump can operate the fountain. The biological filter pumps the water through bacteria-containing layers, the bacteria within them digesting waste organic matter and algae turning it into harmless material. Although the pump may be immersed, the biological filter also involves a large box which must be concealed somewhere away from the pool – not easy if it is in the centre of a paved courtyard. A third device used to attempt to clear green water is the ultraviolet water clarifier which passes the water through a chamber in which it is exposed to UV rays which kill the algal cells. Suffice it to say that none of the methods used will guarantee clear, algae-free water. All require routine attention and, while I wouldn't deny their value for specialized situations such as Koi carp pools, I can't be convinced that they are worthwhile for the average ornamental garden pool.

Blanket weed can be a problem and is best removed immediately

MARGINALS

Acorus calamus Sweet flag

" *This is an odd plant and no mistake, looking for all the world like one of the irises and sharing one of their common names, flag. But the affinities of this native of Asia and North America (although widely naturalized in Europe) are with arums and their kin. History relates that the foliage was used to cover the floors of castles before carpets, and it would have made a good choice, for the 'sweet' epithet of the common name alludes to the pleasant aroma, variously described as of citrus or cinnamon, that exudes from the bruised leaves. An oil used in perfumery is also extracted from the rhizome of the plant.* "

FLOWERS Insignificant, greenish-brown in arum-like spikes borne towards the tops of the stems. In warm areas, reddish fruits are formed but these do not occur in Britain.
FOLIAGE Deciduous, iris-like, up to 2.5cm (1in) wide, usually wrinkled and with pronounced mid-rib.
SITE Full sun or very light shade.
PREFERRED WATER DEPTH 8-25cm (3-10in) (rather less than half this for A. *gramineus* which prefers shallower depths).
RECOMMENDED POOL SIZE Medium (A. *calamus*) or small (A. *gramineus*).
SPECIAL REQUIREMENTS None.
HARDINESS Very hardy, tolerating -20°C (-4°F).
SIZE Will attain 1.25 x 75cm (4ft x 30in) after five years; A. *gramineus*, less than half this.

PLANTING
As rhizomes in spring, directly into the soil.
CARE
Cut down dead foliage and flower spike in autumn or, alternatively, in colder areas, in spring.
PROPAGATION
By division in spring.
PROBLEMS
None.

RECOMMENDED VARIETIES
'Variegatus' has gold and cream-striped leaves, less significant flowers and is slower and more compact in growth.

Acorus calamus

SIMILAR SPECIES
Acorus gramineus (Japanese rush – another misnomer) is a smaller, neater plant with almost grass-like leaves, which also exists in a variegated form, 'Variegatus', sometimes seen as a houseplant.

Alisma plantago-aquatica Water plantain

" *As its common name suggests, the foliage of* Alisma *does indeed look like that of a plantain that has somehow become lost and ended up in a pool. The appearance of the flowers, however, confirms that there is no relationship with real plantains; nor indeed is there any with* Gypsophila, *which is what the feathery blossom most suggests. Alismas should be planted with caution for they can self-seed with wicked abandon. In a wilder garden, the seedheads are welcome as bird food but in smaller, more kempt surroundings, the flower spikes are best cut back before the seeds are set, so as to limit the spread. The entire plant has an acrid smell and can be poisonous; certainly a sedative drug was formerly extracted from the roots.* "

PLANTING
As plants in spring, directly into soil in large pools or in planting baskets.
CARE
Cut down dead flower spikes immediately after flowering in all except

large, wild gardens and cut back dead foliage in autumn.

PROPAGATION

By division in spring, or by seed (most readily by the removal of self-sown seedlings).

PROBLEMS

None.

FLOWERS Small, white, pink or purplish in large, feathery inflorescences.

FOLIAGE Deciduous, plantain-like, broadly elliptical on stalks emerging above water surface.

SITE Full sun.

PREFERRED WATER DEPTH 15-25cm (6-10in) (approximately half of this for A. lanceolatum).

RECOMMENDED POOL SIZE Large or medium.

SPECIAL REQUIREMENTS None.

HARDINESS Very hardy, tolerating -20°C (-4°F).

SIZE Will attain 75 x 45cm (30 x 18in) after two or three years; A. lanceolatum, rather less.

Alisma plantago-aquatica

SIMILAR SPECIES

Alisma lanceolatum is smaller with narrower, more grass-like foliage.

RECOMMENDED VARIETIES

Normal species is usually the only form available although var. *parviflorum* is sometimes seen; it is much smaller, with smaller, pink flowers.

Butomus umbellatus Flowering rush

❝ *Like so many water plants, this one also has a common name that serves to mislead. It isn't a rush and even if it were, so what, for they have flowers too. I wish it was called the umbrella plant as that would more accurately convey its appearance as the stately flower stems arise above the water surface; but the name umbrella plant is already in use for several other things.* ❞

PLANTING

As plants in spring, directly into soil in large pools or in planting baskets.

CARE

Cut down dead flower spikes and leaves in autumn. Divide approximately every three or four years if in fairly confined space.

PROPAGATION

By division in spring, by seed in summer, or by removal of root bulbils where these are accessible.

PROBLEMS

Aphids.

Butomus umbellatus

FLOWERS In summer, fairly large and pink, in attractive spreading umbels.

FOLIAGE Deciduous, narrow, rush-like and twisted, greenish purple with sharp edges.

SITE Full sun to very light shade.

PREFERRED WATER DEPTH 2.5-15cm (1-6in).

RECOMMENDED POOL SIZE Large or medium.

SPECIAL REQUIREMENTS None.

HARDINESS Very hardy, tolerating -20°C (-4°F).

SIZE Will attain 1.25m x 50cm (4ft x 20in) after about two or three years.

RECOMMENDED VARIETIES

Normal species only is available.

MARGINALS

Calla palustris
Bog Arum

❝ Although there are many water-loving members of the family Araceae, I have always considered this one to be the real aquatic equivalent to the common woodland lords and ladies, Arum maculatum. It is seen fairly commonly in the temperate regions of the northern hemisphere, where its rich and glossy, dark green leaves emerge from the mud at pond edges. It has been quite widely naturalized in Britain since the mid-nineteenth century. The small, but typically aroid (arum-type) flower heads are said to be pollinated by water snails and, late in the season, they give rise to rather appealing, bright red fruiting heads. ❞

PLANTING
As rhizomes in spring, directly into soil in large pools; in baskets in smaller ones.

CARE
Little needed once established but dead foliage should be cut back in autumn and winter.

PROPAGATION
By wholesale division or by simply breaking off pieces of the rhizome in spring; also propagated by seed sown fresh in early autumn directly into wet soil.

PROBLEMS
None.

RECOMMENDED VARIETIES
Normal species only is available.

FLOWERS Tiny, in spring on green and white arum-like spadix borne in a white, rather papery spathe. Fruits, round, bright red on short spikes.

FOLIAGE Deciduous or more or less evergreen, rich, glossy green, broadly heart-shaped with long stalk.

SITE Full sun or very light shade.

PREFERRED WATER DEPTH 5-25cm (2-10in).

RECOMMENDED POOL SIZE Medium or large.

SPECIAL REQUIREMENTS None.

HARDINESS Very hardy, tolerating -20°C (-4°F).

SIZE Will attain 25-30 x 25-30cm (10-12 x 10-12in) after two or three years.

SIMILAR SPECIES
Zantedeschia is similar; see p.36.

Calla palustris

Caltha palustris
Marsh Marigold, Kingcup

❝ Perhaps the most familiar and most loved native British water-side plant, this is a beautiful water buttercup of imposing proportions, both in its flowers and its leaves. Much of its appeal to me lies in the neatness of its clumps; it never becomes unkempt and straggly in the way of so many true buttercup species. Caltha has several interesting flower variants and I am always intrigued by the way that they divide gardeners' opinions. Even Miss Jekyll herself pronounced on her preference for the singles. ❞

PLANTING
As plants in spring, directly into soil.

CARE
Little needed once established but dead foliage may be cut back and the plants generally tidied up in autumn. In more formal plantings, best divided every four or five years.

PROPAGATION
By division in spring, or by seed sown fresh in early autumn in wet soil.

PROBLEMS
Aphids, mildew.

RECOMMENDED VARIETIES
My strong preference is for the golden-yellow, single flowered normal species but others opt for the highly floriferous and tightly double flowered 'Flore Pleno' or the single white 'Alba'.

Caltha palustris

FLOWERS Golden-yellow, buttercup-like in spring; also occurs in double and white flowered variants.
FOLIAGE Deciduous, more or less rounded, dark green and very glossy, long-stalked.
SITE Prefers full sun or light to medium shade; often found naturally in waterlogged woodland soils.
PREFERRED WATER DEPTH 0-15cm (0-6in).
RECOMMENDED POOL SIZE Preferably medium or large; may be planted as single specimens alongside small pools but doesn't look as effective as in a massed planting.
SPECIAL REQUIREMENTS None.
HARDINESS Very hardy, tolerating -20°C (-4°F).
SIZE Will attain 60 x 50cm (24 x 20in) within three or four years; the double flowered 'Flore Pleno' about half this.

Cotula coronopifolia
Brass buttons

" At least the name is descriptive, for this tiny aquatic South African daisy does have small, button-like flowers. This is a useful plant for the edges of small, informal pools, partly as it is not very invasive, and because it can't become out of hand as it isn't very long lived, nor very hardy and in cold winters will die, to be renewed again in spring. "

PLANTING
As plants in spring, directly into soil.
CARE
None normally needed although, in milder areas where it is truly perennial, it may with advantage be divided every three or four years.
PROPAGATION
By division in spring, or by seed sown in spring in wet soil.
PROBLEMS
None.

FLOWERS Golden-yellow, rounded, button-like for a long period in summer.
FOLIAGE Deciduous, small, narrowly elongated, mid-green, sparsely toothed.
SITE Full sun or very light shade.
PREFERRED WATER DEPTH 0-10cm (0-4in).
RECOMMENDED POOL SIZE Small.
SPECIAL REQUIREMENTS None.
HARDINESS Moderately hardy, tolerating -10°C (14°F).
SIZE Will attain about 15 x 30cm (6 x 12in) after two or three years in mild areas.

Cotula coronopifolia

MARGINALS

Equisetum hyemale
Scouring rush

❝ *I have been addicted to horsetails ever since my days at primary school when I first learned of the Carboniferous period, for there is something rather special about a plant that has changed little in general form for over two hundred million years. It was ancient relatives of the modern-day species of* Equisetum *that populated the coal-forming swamps in the company of primitive reptiles and amphibians. That one of their number is still in the company of the frogs of my garden pool is, therefore, entirely appropriate. Of the numerous extant species, this one,* E. hyemale, *is the best one for a pool. The common name of 'scouring rush' comes from the plant's traditional use as a pot scourer, its silica encrusted tissues working as well as many a present-day abrasive.* ❞

PLANTING
As plants in autumn or spring, directly into soil in large pools; in baskets in smaller ones.

CARE
Little needed, but dead stems may be cut out as necessary (don't pull them as this may result in cut fingers).

PROPAGATION
By division in spring.

PROBLEMS
None.

FLOWERS None, but small greenish 'cones' at tips of stems.
FOLIAGE Evergreen, true leaves tiny and sheath-like around joints of the finely fluted, mainly unbranched green stems.
SITE Full sun to moderate shade.
PREFERRED WATER DEPTH 5-20cm (2-8in).
RECOMMENDED POOL SIZE Small to large.
SPECIAL REQUIREMENTS None.
HARDINESS Hardy to very hardy, tolerating -15 to -20°C (5 to -4°F).
SIZE 1-1.5m x 25cm (3-5ft x 10in) after two or three years.

RECOMMENDED VARIETIES
Normal species only is available.

Equisetum hyemale

Houttuynia cordata

❝ *By and large, I like plants with variegated foliage, but I'm not entirely sure about this one. It has a variety called 'Chameleon', the main reason for its present popularity, that really seems to have just too many colours for its own good. It is an oriental, rather aromatic plant with a peculiar smell, somewhat reminiscent of citrus fruit. Perhaps I am painting too unappetizing a picture, however, for it seems to be the* sine qua non *of modern water gardens; although I still don't have it in mine.* ❞

FLOWERS White, tiny, in early summer, in cone-shaped spikes surrounded by greenish-white bracts.
FOLIAGE Deciduous or more or less evergreen leaves, more or less oval, greenish-blue with reddish margins and red stems.
SITE Light to moderate shade (best planted beneath dappled shade of larger leaved plants).
PREFERRED WATER DEPTH 0-10cm (0-4in).
RECOMMENDED POOL SIZE Small to large.
SPECIAL REQUIREMENTS None.
HARDINESS Hardy to very hardy, tolerating -15 to -20°C (5 to 14°F).
SIZE 30 x 50cm (12 x 20in) after three or four years.

Houttuynia cordata

PLANTING
As plants in autumn or spring, directly into soil in large pools; in baskets in smaller ones.

CARE
Little needed, but foliage may be tidied up in autumn in more formal settings. Divide approximately every three or four years.

PROPAGATION
By division in spring.

PROBLEMS
None.

RECOMMENDED VARIETIES
The normal species with rather bluish-green leaves is infrequently seen, the multi-coloured variety, 'Chameleon' with red, cream, white and green-variegated leaves being much more common. 'Flore Pleno' has double flowers.

Hypericum elodes
Marsh St John's Wort

" Most hypericums are border shrubs of variable merit. This western European species is a creeping herbaceous perennial, also of slightly variable merit, for hypericum flowers are never exciting at the best of times. But for a fairly large planting, where it can make a small contribution to an overall effect, it is probably a plant worth having. "

RECOMMENDED VARIETIES
Normal species only is available.

PLANTING
As plants in autumn or spring, directly into soil in large pools; in baskets in smaller ones.

CARE
Little needed once established but it may be necessary to tidy up the foliage in autumn.

FLOWERS Yellow, small, appearing in summer.
FOLIAGE Deciduous, small, oval pale green leaves on densely white woolly-looking stems.
SITE Full sun to light shade.
PREFERRED WATER DEPTH 0-8cm (0-3in).
RECOMMENDED POOL SIZE Small to medium.
SPECIAL REQUIREMENTS None.
HARDINESS Moderately hardy, tolerating -10 to -20°C (14 to -4°F).
SIZE 20 x 50cm (8 x 20in) after three or four years.

PROPAGATION
By division in spring, or by removal of rooted layers.

PROBLEMS
None.

Hypericum elodes

MARGINALS

Water irises

❝ It seems likely that the genus Iris *contains species appropriate to a wider range of garden habitats than almost any other. From tiny rock garden bulbs to giant border perennials, there's an iris for almost every situation. And so, there are irises for the water garden too. On p.82, I've described the species that are happiest in the bog garden; here I shall concentrate on those that really prefer to have their rhizomes in water:* Iris ensata *and* I. laevigata *are Oriental,* I. pseudacorus *is European and* I. versicolor *North American. All have the readily recognizable iris flowers, but I do urge you to be adventurous and not simply accept the varieties that are stocked everywhere – it really will be worth the effort of going to a specialist supplier. ❞*

PLANTING
Ideally as newly sprouting rhizomes in spring although there is also much to be said for buying your plants later when you can see the flower colours. Plant directly into soil in large pools; in baskets in smaller ones.

CARE
Cut back dead flower spikes by cutting at an angle flush with the first sheathing leaf. Cut back old foliage as it discolours in autumn. Divide every three or four years in spring.

PROPAGATION
By division in spring.

PROBLEMS
Aphids, snails.

FLOWERS Familiar and characteristic with three outer parts or falls that hang downwards, and three inner parts or standards, more or less upright. Falls are often marked with contrasting colours. Some species have one flower per stem, others several.
FOLIAGE Deciduous or evergreen, narrow and sword-like with sheathing base.
SITE Full sun to light shade.
PREFERRED WATER DEPTH 2.5-15cm (1-6in), preferably rather less in summer.

RECOMMENDED POOL SIZE Small to large, depending on vigour; *I. pseudacorus* is suitable only for larger pools.
SPECIAL REQUIREMENTS None.
HARDINESS Hardy, tolerating -15°C (5°F); *I. pseudacorus* very hardy, tolerating -20°C (-4°F).
SIZE Varies with species and variety from about 60 x 20cm (2 x 8in) after two years for some of the *I. laevigata* varieties to 2 x 1m (6 x 3ft) for *I. pseudacorus* which does become a very large plant.

RECOMMENDED VARIETIES

Iris ensata (syn. *I. kaempferi*) (reddish-purple), 'Alba' (white), 'Higo' hybrids, (a range including blue, mauve, pink and white, often with flecks and spots), 'Moonlight Waves' (white with greenish centre), 'Rose Queen' (pink), 'Variegata' (purple, leaves striped white). *I. laevigata* (bluish-violet), 'Alba' (white), 'Atro-purpurea' (red-purple), 'Colchesterensis' (white with dark blue centre), 'Midnight' (dark blue with white markings), 'Variegata' (pale blue, leaves striped white). *I. pseudacorus* (yellow flag iris) (yellow), 'Alba' (white), *bastardii* (pale yellow), 'Variegata' (golden-yellow, leaves with golden stripes early in season). *I. versicolor* (red-purple or mauve with darker and white markings), 'Kermesina' (red-purple).

Iris ensata

Iris pseudacorus

Iris laevigata 'Variegata'

Lobelia cardinalis

❝ *This will come as a surprise to those gardeners used to thinking of lobelias as the mainly blue-flowered, half-hardy, South African summer bedding plants that tumble from hanging baskets and spill over the edges of beds. For this plant is hardier (although not totally tough), aquatic, tall and has red flowers, but a lobelia it certainly is – a North American member of what is a huge genus of over 300 species ranging from tiny annuals to small trees. Lobelia cardinalis is a pool-side gem and in areas where it isn't fully hardy, it should be grown in containers and taken under shelter in the winter.* ❞

PLANTING
As plants in spring, contained in planting baskets.

CARE
Cut back dead flower stems and old foliage in autumn. Lift complete in baskets if necessary, put into larger containers and keep under cover in a greenhouse over winter.

PROPAGATION
By division in spring, also by layering or leaf-bud cuttings in summer.

PROBLEMS
Aphids, fungal leaf spots, snails.

SIMILAR SPECIES
Lobelia fulgens, also from North America, is similar but more graceful. *L. dortmanna* is a more or less submerged rosette-forming species (see p.56).

Lobelia cardinalis 'Queen Victoria'

FLOWERS Rich red, in tall spikes, in summer; in form rather like those of a salvia but with very much more class.
FOLIAGE Deciduous, narrowly elongated, reddish-bronze.
SITE Full sun to light shade.
PREFERRED WATER DEPTH 0-10cm (0-4in).
RECOMMENDED POOL SIZE Small to large.
SPECIAL REQUIREMENTS Lift for indoor storage in winter in all except very mild areas.
HARDINESS Fairly hardy, tolerating -5 to -10°C (23-14°F).
SIZE Will attain 1m x 25cm (3ft x 10in) after three years.

RECOMMENDED VARIETIES
The normal species is most frequently seen although there are several rather similar hybrids with *Lobelia cardinalis* as one of the parents. Of these 'Queen Victoria', with blood-red foliage, is particularly fine and fairly easily obtained.

MARGINALS

Mentha aquatica Water mint

❝ *An abiding memory of student field trips to study the ecology of bogs and marshes is the smell of mint. It came from walking along the edges of pools and ditches and unavoidably trampling* Mentha aquatica *beneath my boots. Like most terrestrial mints, it is a vigorous, invasive plant. In the larger water garden, however, this native European plant is an indispensable component.* ❞

FLOWERS Characteristic of most mints; pale mauve and massed in rather large heads at the ends of the shoots.
FOLIAGE Deciduous, more or less oval, toothed, generally rather woolly-hairy, dark green on green-purple, creeping stems.
SITE Full sun to moderate shade; water mint is among the more shade tolerant aquatic plants and in the wild it scrambles beneath other vegetation.
PREFERRED WATER DEPTH 2.5-15cm (1-6in).
RECOMMENDED POOL SIZE Medium to large.
SPECIAL REQUIREMENTS In all except the largest pools, must be lifted and divided quite frequently.
HARDINESS Very hardy, tolerating -20°C (-4°F).
SIZE Will attain about 1m x 75cm (3ft x 30in) within about two years.

Mentha aquatica

PLANTING
As plants in spring or possibly in autumn. May be planted directly into soil in very large pools but it is so invasive that it is always better in planting baskets.

CARE
Cut back dead stems in autumn and, in all except the largest pools, lift and divide every two or three years to keep within bounds.

PROPAGATION
By division in spring, by stem cuttings in spring or summer, or from seed sown in spring.

PROBLEMS
Mildew, rust (although I find it appearing much less frequently on *M. aquatica* than on some of the herb garden mints).

RECOMMENDED VARIETIES
Normal species only is available.

Menyanthes trifoliata Bog bean

❝ Menyanthes *isn't a true, leguminous bean but it does have three-lobed leaves very reminiscent of those of the broad bean, although there the resemblance ends for the flowers and fruits are quite dissimilar. I consider it to be among the more attractive marginals, for the smooth, rather pale green leaves have a graceful simplicity as they emerge from the water at the pool's edge. It is, nonetheless, a somewhat invasive species and is, therefore, a bit of a risk in smaller water gardens. Its rather 'soft' appearance belies a tough character, for this is a very hardy plant indeed from northern temperate regions. I'm told that in some parts of northern Europe an alcoholic drink is prepared from the roots.* ❞

PLANTING
As young plants in spring, most satisfactorily directly into the soil but may be grown in planting baskets in smaller pools.

CARE
Cut back dead shoots in autumn; divide every three or four years.

PROPAGATION
By division in spring.

PROBLEMS
None.

RECOMMENDED VARIETIES
Normal species only is available.

FLOWERS Small, star-like, pinkish-white in summer in loose heads borne most attractively above the water surface. For this reason, the plant is, I think, better grown in several centimetres of water rather than at the margin itself.

FOLIAGE Deciduous, three-lobed leaves with three smooth, neatly rounded segments.

SITE Full sun.

PREFERRED WATER DEPTH 2.5-25cm (1-10in).

RECOMMENDED POOL SIZE Medium to large.

SPECIAL REQUIREMENTS None.

HARDINESS Very hardy, tolerating -20°C (-4°F).

SIZE Will attain about 75 x 50cm (30 x 20in) after two or three years.

Mimulus luteus

Mimulus Musk

❝ Mimulus *flowers are fairly familiar, and are seen growing alongside ditches and pools in North America and also in parts of Europe where they have become naturalized. Of the common species that are most at home in an aquatic habitat (for there are more terrestrial, border forms too), one,* Mimulus moschatus, *has an extraordinary history for it was once one of the most richly perfumed of garden flowers but, mysteriously, throughout the world, all strains of the plants lost much of their aroma around the year 1914 and have never recovered it. But, even if you are a* Mimulus *lover; don't plant them in any other than large water gardens for most are fairly invasive and will self-seed.* ❞

FLOWERS Characteristically two-lipped, rather like snapdragons (*Antirrhinum*), usually yellow, orange or red but sometimes bluish; generally borne in abundance over the plants and sometimes in tall spikes.

FOLIAGE Deciduous, rather small, mid-green, fairly rounded and sometimes toothed leaves on creeping stems.

SITE Full sun to light or more moderate shade.

PREFERRED WATER DEPTH Varies with species, most preferring from 0-7.5cm (0-3in) but a few, including *M. ringens*, prefer a depth of 7.5-15cm (3-6in).

RECOMMENDED POOL SIZE Medium to large.

SPECIAL REQUIREMENTS None.

HARDINESS Very hardy, tolerating -20°C (-4°F).

SIZE Varies with species; most of the more or less creeping forms will attain from 30-45 x 50cm (12-18 x 20in) after three or four years but the more upright *M. lewisii* and *M. ringens* will reach double this height.

PLANTING
As plants in spring, either directly into soil or into planting baskets.

CARE
Cut back dead shoots in autumn; divide every two or three years.

PROPAGATION
By division in spring, by softwood cuttings in summer, or from seed in spring (some forms).

PROBLEMS
Fungal rots, especially *Botrytis* (grey mould).

RECOMMENDED VARIETIES
Mimulus luteus (water musk, yellow musk) yellow flowers with red blotches, from mid- to late summer. *M. ringens* (lavender musk) bluish flowers, summer. *M. moschatus* (monkey musk), yellow flowers, summer. *M. lewisii* (great purple monkey flower), pink to purple-red flowers, summer. A hybrid derived from it, *M. x bartonianus*, is similar.

MARGINALS

Myosotis scorpioides
Water forget-me-not

❝ *There are aquatic versions of many plants that we tend to think of purely as normal garden subjects and the forget-me-not is no exception. Indeed, many forget-me-nots revel in hot, dry conditions and many are annual or biennial so it's a surprise to discover this perennial European species that enjoys having its roots in the water. But it is a pleasant surprise for this is unmistakably a real forget-me-not with its cheerful, tiny blue flowers.* ❞

Myosotis scorpioides

PLANTING
As plants in spring or possibly in autumn. It is best planted directly into the soil as, although creeping, it is never unduly invasive.

CARE
Cut back dead stems in autumn and, if necessary, lift and divide every two or three years.

FLOWERS In summer, small, round, single, bright blue with central eye in contrasting white, pink or yellow.
FOLIAGE Deciduous, small, usually hairy, elongated-oval, bright green leaves on long trailing stems.
SITE Full sun to moderate shade; probably the most shade tolerant of all freely-flowering water plants.
PREFERRED WATER DEPTH 0-10cm (0-4in).
RECOMMENDED POOL SIZE Small to large.
SPECIAL REQUIREMENTS None.
HARDINESS Very hardy, tolerating -20°C (-4°F).
SIZE Will attain about 25 x 60cm (10 x 24in) within two years. The stems are much longer than this but trail and flop.

RECOMMENDED VARIETIES
The normal species is the form seen most often but the selected varieties, 'Mermaid' (particularly large, bright blue flowers that flower for longer) and 'Pinkie' (pink flowers) may also be found.

PROPAGATION
By division in spring, by removal of rooted rhizomes or, with the true species, by removal of any self-sown seedlings.

PROBLEMS
Mildew, aphids.

Peltandra undulata (syn. virginica)
Arrow arum

❝ *Yet another member of that invaluable water plant family, the Araceae, peltandras are North American species with especially fine, glossy, arrow-like leaves. They are particularly valuable as members of mixed foliage plantings along the margins of medium to large pools. Because they are individually fairly large and because they do look their best in big groups, however, they really aren't species most suitable for small water gardens.* ❞

FLOWERS In late spring, typically aroid, tiny on a short spadix rather closely embraced by the green and white sheathing spathe.
FOLIAGE More or less evergreen, spear- or arrow-shaped, rich glossy green, elongating after the flowers fade. Spike of greenish berries.
SITE Full sun to light shade.
PREFERRED WATER DEPTH 0-25cm (0-10in).
RECOMMENDED POOL SIZE Medium to large.
SPECIAL REQUIREMENTS None.
HARDINESS Hardy, tolerating about -15°C (5°F).
SIZE Will attain about 75 x 45cm (30 x 18in) after two or three years.

Peltandra undulata (syn. virginica)

PLANTING

As plants or rhizomes in spring, preferably directly into the soil; if they need to be confined to baskets, then the pool is probably too small for them.

CARE

Little needed, but dead and dying foliage should be cut back in autumn. In cold areas, it may be advantageous to pack bracken or similar material around the crown for protection in winter where the rhizomes are not covered with water.

PROPAGATION

By division of rhizomes in spring.

PROBLEMS

None.

RECOMMENDED VARIETIES

Normal species only is available.

Ranunculus Spearwort

❝ *The water-loving buttercup-like plants of the Ranunculaceae seem to be taking progressive steps into the water garden. Caltha palustris (p.24) is really happiest just above the margin, Ranunculus aquatilis is most at home when submerged on a stream bed, while the two European and Asian species of spearwort lie somewhere in between in shallow water. They are unmistakably buttercups, with their cheerful yellow flowers, but as their name suggests, they have elongated spear-like leaves. I always think they have rather a lot of leaf in relation to the size and number of flowers but they are pretty enough in a mixed planting.* ❞

Ranunculus lingua

FLOWERS In summer, single, yellow, buttercup-like, solitary or in small heads at ends of stems.
FOLIAGE Deciduous, elongated, spear-shaped green leaves.
SITE Full sun to very light shade.
PREFERRED WATER DEPTH 0-10cm (0-4in).
RECOMMENDED POOL SIZE Medium to large, although *R. flammula* is also suitable for small pools.
SPECIAL REQUIREMENTS None.
HARDINESS Very hardy, tolerating -20°C (-4°F).
SIZE *R. lingua* will attain about 1m x 25cm (3ft x 10in) after two or three years; *R. flammula* little more than a third of this.

PLANTING

As plants in spring, preferably directly into the soil but they may also be planted in baskets in smaller pools.

CARE

Cut back dead and dying foliage in autumn. May be divided every three or four years if spreading widely.

PROPAGATION

By division in spring. Also from seed sown in spring.

PROBLEMS

Mildew.

RECOMMENDED VARIETIES

Ranunculus flammula, normal species only is available. *R. lingua*, a variety with showy flowers called 'Grandiflorus' is also seen.

MARGINALS

Sagittaria sagittifolia Arrowhead

❝ *This isn't the only arrowhead in the water garden (*Peltandra *p.32 is another) but, while peltandras are American, the common hardy sagittarias are very much Old World species and one of them,* Sagittaria sagittifolia, *is one of the more robust and common of native British water-side plants. The leaves are beautiful and well justify their common name but the plant is invasive and should be planted with caution. In larger pools, it tends to be attacked by ducks which eat the tubers; hence the colloquial name 'duck potato'.* ❞

Sagittaria sagittifolia

PLANTING

As plants or tubers in spring or possibly in autumn. It is best planted directly into the soil by large pools or in large baskets although it really is too vigorous to be properly confined. It may also be grown as a submerged and floating plant by weighting the

FLOWERS In summer, rather large, white, with a dark purple blotch at the base of the petals.
FOLIAGE Deciduous, with three types of leaf: large, green, glossy and arrowhead-shaped aerial leaves on plants growing as marginals; more or less oval, floating leaves; and elongated, submerged leaves produced when submerged tubers first begin growth in the spring.
SITE Full sun to very light shade.
PREFERRED WATER DEPTH 0-10cm (0-4in) (as marginal) but also up to 60cm (24in) as submerged aquatic.
RECOMMENDED POOL SIZE Medium to large.
SPECIAL REQUIREMENTS None.
HARDINESS Hardy, tolerating -15 to -20°C (5 to 4°F).
SIZE Will attain about 50 x 30cm (20 x 12in) in two years.

tubers and dropping them into deeper water.

CARE
Cut back dead stems in autumn and, if necessary, lift and divide every two or three years.

PROPAGATION
By division in spring, by removal and replanting of the overwintering tubers that develop at the tips of the runners in late autumn, or by seed in the spring.

PROBLEMS
Aphids.

Typha Reedmace

❝ *The baby Moses was never hidden among a clump of typhas, although you might be forgiven for thinking otherwise as both classical and modern illustrations of the Old Testament story often depict their unmistakable club-like heads and they have, indeed, become popularly known as bulrushes. In reality, the name bulrush is more accurately applied to a species of* Scirpus *and also to the warm-climate* Cyperus papyrus *which was probably the plant that provided Moses with his protection.* Typha, *more usefully and unambiguously called the reedmace, is, however, one of the most stately of temperate water-side genera but almost all are truly invasive and should only be planted beside really large pools. Only* T. minima *should be considered for planting in smaller water gardens.* ❞

PLANTING
As plants in spring or possibly in autumn; best planted directly into the soil by large pools or in large baskets although, with the exception of *T. minima*, they are really too vigorous to be properly confined.

FLOWERS In summer, tiny, in brown, velvety rod or tail-like heads with males above females; in some species the two parts are quite distinct (see Recommended Varieties).

FOLIAGE Deciduous or more or less evergreen, leaves green or grey-green, tough, grass-like, usually embracing the stem and often curiously spongy at the base.

SITE Full sun to very light shade.

PREFERRED WATER DEPTH 0-15cm (0-6in).

RECOMMENDED POOL SIZE Large (except *T. minima*, small or medium).

SPECIAL REQUIREMENTS Take care when planting in pools with butyl or other rubber liners because the tips of the rhizomes, on the larger species especially, are needle-like and will readily cause punctures.

HARDINESS Very hardy, tolerating -20°C (-4°F).

SIZE Varies with species: *T. latifolia* will attain 2.5-3m x 50-75cm (8 x 10ft x 20-30in) after two or three years, *T. angustifolia* two-thirds and *T. laxmannii* one-third of this; *T. mimina* will only reach an approximate height of 45 x 20cm (18 x 8in).

Typha latifolia

Typha minima

CARE

Cut back dead foliage in autumn. Ideally, the club-like seedheads should also be cut back before they disperse their seeds although, unfortunately, they are the plant's chief attraction.

PROPAGATION

By division in spring, or by removal of the self-sown seedlings.

PROBLEMS

Aphids.

Typha angustifolia

RECOMMENDED VARIETIES

Typha latifolia (great reedmace), a huge species with massive, poker-like, flower heads. *T. angustifolia* (lesser reedmace), smaller but still a large plant with club-like heads of female flowers separated by a gap from the tail-like male heads above. *T. laxmannii*, medium-sized with slender female flower heads topped with tail-like male heads. *T. minima*, the smallest species with neat, spherical heads of female flowers topped with a small 'tail'.

MARGINALS

Veronica beccabunga Brooklime

❝ *I always see this plant in my mind's eye rather as I see* Myosotis scorpioides *for they do, indeed, have much in common. Both have very pretty, small blue flowers, both have a creeping habit and both are water-loving versions of plants that we know more familiarly in terrestrial, even dry habitats. For while the* Myosotis *is a water forget-me-not, this* Veronica *is an aquatic speedwell. In reality,* Veronica *is much the larger genus, embracing around 250 species and* V. beccabunga *isn't the only aquatic although it is far and away the commonest offered for cultivation. The 'lime' of the common name seems to be derived from an old observed association of the plant with brooks in chalky places.* **❞**

PLANTING
As plants in spring, ideally into planting baskets.

CARE
Little is needed once fully established, although in small pools, dead stems may be trimmed right back in the autumn.

PROPAGATION
By division in spring, by softwood cuttings in summer, by removal of naturally rooted runners, or by seed in spring.

PROBLEMS
Mildew.

RECOMMENDED VARIETIES
Normal species only is available.

FLOWERS In summer, small, round, single, vivid blue with a tiny white eye although the blue is somewhat variable in intensity.
FOLIAGE Deciduous, small, more or less rounded, rather fleshy green leaves on long creeping stems.
SITE Full sun to moderate shade.
PREFERRED WATER DEPTH 0-10cm (0-4in).
RECOMMENDED POOL SIZE Small to large.
SPECIAL REQUIREMENTS None.
HARDINESS Very hardy, tolerating -20°C (-4°F).
SIZE Will attain about 15 x 45cm (6 x 18in) in two years.

Veronica beccabunga

Zantedeschia aethiopica

❝ *This aroid is sometimes confusingly called the Calla lily, but although it is certainly no lily, it can with justification be considered a warm climate version of* Calla. *Despite its specific name, it originates in South Africa although it now grows widely throughout warm parts of the world. Its white aroid (arum-like) spathe is probably best known as a cut flower and many variously coloured hybrids have been derived from it specifically for the floristry trade.* **❞**

PLANTING
As rhizomes or young plants in the spring, put directly into soil in very mild areas, otherwise contained within planting baskets or submerged pots.

CARE
In all except mild areas, lift in autumn and pot up for storing with greenhouse or other protection in winter. In mild areas, ensure that crowns are covered by at least 25cm (10in) of water or, alternatively, pack bracken, straw or other protective covering over them.

PROPAGATION
By division or by careful removal of pieces of sprouting rhizome in spring; also by seed in spring.

PROBLEMS
Fungal leaf spot.

SIMILAR SPECIES
Calla is similar; see p.24.

FLOWERS Tiny in spring on a yellow, arum-like spadix borne in a spreading white spathe. Fruits are round, orange on short spikes but not always formed in cooler climates.
FOLIAGE Deciduous or more or less evergreen, rich, glossy green, broadly heart-shaped with long stalk.
SITE Full sun or moderate shade.
PREFERRED WATER DEPTH 5-25cm (2-10in).
RECOMMENDED POOL SIZE Medium or large.
SPECIAL REQUIREMENTS Should be lifted in autumn for winter storage.
HARDINESS Fairly hardy, tolerating -5 to -10°C (23 to 14°F).
SIZE Will attain 30-45 x 25-30cm (12-18 x 10-12in) after two or three years, although may be considerably taller when in the shade of other plants.

RECOMMENDED VARIETIES
The normal species is the form most frequently seen as a water garden plant although the slightly more vigorous variety, 'Crowborough', is better, having been selected for its greater hardiness. The striking 'Green Goddess' has a green and white spathe and is another outdoor form although slightly more tender, but the many named and coloured hybrids are not really suitable for outdoor pool cultivation in Europe.

Zantedeschia aethiopica 'Green Goddess'

Zantedeschia aethiopica 'Crowborough'

WATER PLANTS

Aponogeton distachyos
Water hawthorn, Cape pondweed

❝ The name 'Cape pondweed' I can understand for this is a plant that grows in ponds and originates in South Africa. 'Water hawthorn' is more obscure; I can only assume it refers to the sweetly scented flowers. Nonetheless, the fact that Aponogeton does have an appealing scent is a very desirable bonus as is the even rarer attribute that in milder areas it will produce its flowers during the winter. A fair degree of shade tolerance adds further to this being one of the very best and most choice of water plants. ❞

Aponogeton distachyos

PLANTING
As tubers or plants in spring, ideally into planting baskets.

CARE
Little needed once established although dead foliage should be pulled out if possible in autumn.

FLOWERS In late spring and in autumn, also winter in mild areas; white with dark, almost black anthers, and arranged on a forked stalk. Fruit ripen below water and then float to disperse seeds when they may be collected by net.

FOLIAGE Deciduous in most temperate areas but more or less evergreen in mild places; elongated-oval, mid-green, floating leaves.

SITE Full sun to moderate shade.

PREFERRED WATER DEPTH 25-60cm (10-24in).

RECOMMENDED POOL SIZE Medium to large.

SPECIAL REQUIREMENTS None.

HARDINESS Fairly hardy, tolerating about -5°C (23°F) but safely surviving cold winters in a dormant state in deep water.

SIZE Will attain a spread at water surface of about 1 x 1m (3 x 3ft) after three years.

RECOMMENDED VARIETIES
The normal species only is available although a pinkish-flowered form does exist.

PROPAGATION
By division in spring, or by seed, ideally sown fresh in autumn into submerged pots.

PROBLEM
None.

Hippuris vulgaris
Mare's tail

❝ In anticipation of some of the comments that I might receive, no, I'm not suggesting that you plant one of the most ineradicable of weeds in your garden pool. That is horsetail, Equisetum vulgare; this is mare's tail, Hippuris vulgaris, although to confuse you even further, there are aquatic species of Equisetum and one of them I do, indeed, recommend (p.26). But back to Hippuris, which is a native European plant that seems to figure rather infrequently in books on water gardening. This can only be because it is not considered sufficiently meritorious, but I find this a strange conclusion, for its Christmas tree-like form has a special and unusual appeal of which I am very fond. It is tolerant of a wide range of water conditions and may also be grown as a marginal. ❞

PLANTING
As plants or rhizomes in spring, ideally into large planting baskets.

CARE
Little needed once established although dead foliage should be pulled out if possible in autumn.

PROPAGATION
By division in spring.

PROBLEMS
None.

RECOMMENDED VARIETIES
Normal species only is available.

FLOWERS In summer, minute, green and insignificant.

FOLIAGE Deciduous, in whorls, short and very narrowly strap-like on the emerged parts of the stem; thinner and more flimsy on submerged portions (and then much more reminiscent of a mare's tail).

SITE Full sun to light shade.

PREFERRED WATER DEPTH 5-60cm (2-24in).

RECOMMENDED POOL SIZE Medium to large.

SPECIAL REQUIREMENTS None.

HARDINESS Very hardy, tolerating -20°C (-4°F).

SIZE Varies with depth of water. When grown as a marginal, will only attain about 30cm (12in) in height, but in deeper water will consistently produce shoots that emerge up to about 30cm (12in) above the surface. Spreads to about 45cm (18in) after two or three years.

Hippuris vulgaris

WATER PLANTS

Nuphar Water lily, Pond lily

> Nuphars are lesser known members of the water-lily family, at least to gardeners, although one of the native European species, Nuphar lutea, is much more familiar in the wild. It is a very large, invasive species, with leaves probably bigger than those of any other British plant. It is because of these giant proportions that it should only be planted in the very largest pools and in deep water; in lakes, indeed, rather than in ponds. Apart from its distinctive yellow flowers, the fruits are its most remarkable feature, being markedly flask-shaped and giving rise to one of the common names of 'brandy bottle'. There are, nonetheless, related species with attractive leaf variegations and rather less antisocial dimensions that share a useful degree of shade tolerance. "

RECOMMENDED VARIETIES

Usually, only the normal species of *Nuphar lutea* is available; however, a variegated form is now separated as a distinct species *N. variegata*. The less vigorous *N. japonica* and *N. pumila* are scaled-down versions with few merits over the *Nymphaea* water lilies, but both exist with variegated foliage, a valuable attribute among plants with floating leaves. Both of these forms are not surprisingly called *variegata*.

FLOWERS In summer, yellow, reddish in some species, bottle-shaped, strongly and rather strangely scented.
FOLIAGE Deciduous, circular or more or less oval, mid-green floating leaves (up to 40 x 30cm (16 x 12in) in *N. lutea*); thin, translucent, feathery, submerged leaves.
SITE Full sun to moderate shade.
PREFERRED WATER DEPTH 1-2.5m (3-8ft) (*N. lutea*); 45-55cm (18-22in) (*N. japonica*); 30-45cm (12-18in) (*N. pumila*).
RECOMMENDED POOL SIZE Medium to large (very large only for *N. lutea*).
SPECIAL REQUIREMENTS Deeper water than most other water plants.
HARDINESS Very hardy, tolerating -20°C (-4°F).
SIZE *N. lutea* will attain a spread at water surface of at least 2 x 2m (6 x 6ft) after two years; the other species barely half this.

Nuphar japonica

PLANTING
As rhizomes or young plants in spring; directly into soil in large pools but the smaller species in baskets in smaller ones.

CARE
Little needed although dead foliage should be pulled out, if possible, in autumn when small species are grown in smaller pools.

PROPAGATION
By division in spring.

PROBLEMS
Aphids.

Nuphar lutea

Nymphoides peltata Fringed water lily, floating heart

❝Superficially, very much like a water lily (and also, indeed, a floating heart) but in reality a close relative of the bog bean (p.000), this is a fairly common native plant throughout Europe and Asia and is now rather widely naturalized in North America. Its flowers are pretty enough if you like small yellow blooms, although they don't really stand comparison with real yellow water lilies, either in Nuphar *or* Nymphaea, *but the leaves are extremely pretty and the combination does make for a very appealing, if invasive, plant for bigger pools.❞*

Nymphoides peltata

FLOWERS In summer, yellow, with tiny fringes or frills to each of the petals.
FOLIAGE Deciduous, circular to heart-shaped, mid-green floating leaves.
SITE Full sun to light shade.
PREFERRED WATER DEPTH 15-45cm (6-18in).
RECOMMENDED POOL SIZE Medium to large.
SPECIAL REQUIREMENTS None.
HARDINESS Very hardy, tolerating -20°C (-4°F).
SIZE Will attain a spread at the water surface of about 60 x 60cm (24 x 24in) after two years.

PLANTING

As rhizomes or young plants in the spring; preferably contained within planting baskets.

CARE

Pull out dead foliage in autumn before it sinks and rots.

PROPAGATION

By division in spring.

PROBLEMS

Aphids.

RECOMMENDED VARIETIES

Usually, only the normal species is available although a form called 'Bennettii' is sometimes seen, however this significantly lacks the pretty leaf mottling.

WATER PLANTS

Nymphaea Water lily

The queens of the garden pool by almost anyone's reckoning, water lilies must exist in more flower colours and a greater range of overall vigour than almost any other garden plant. Largely because of the range of colours, which can vary from the most subdued to the most strident, a water lily can affect the overall appearance of your pool to a greater extent than anything else. I have said a water lily, singular rather than plural, quite deliberately because most small pools have room for only one plant. Even in large ones with space for several individuals, you may well share my view that it might be wise to choose all of the same variety because those colours, so numerous and varied, don't always blend well with each other. Indeed, a combination of some of the yellow, red and pink water lilies is as unfortunate a sight as gardening has to offer. And although it is the flowers that first spring to mind when water lilies are discussed, it's worth bearing in mind that some have extremely attractive foliage too.

The wide range of vigour and also of preferred water depth means that the varieties must be selected with considerable care. There are few experiences more frustrating than discovering that, just when your water lily has established itself, the entire water surface of your pool is vanishing beneath its all-covering carpet of foliage.

Nymphaea 'Madame Wilfron Gonnère'

Nymphaea 'Colossea'

Nymphaea 'Gonnère'

Nymphaea 'Masaniello'

Nymphaea 'Moorei'

Nymphaea 'Mrs Richmond'

Nymphaea alba

Nymphaea 'Amabilis'

Nymphaea 'Marliacea Chromatella'

Nymphaea 'Marliacea Rosea'

WATER PLANTS

Nymphaea Water lily (continued)

FLOWERS In summer, each lasting for three or four days only before dipping below the water surface, never to return. The plant as a whole continues blooming for several months. The flowers of most hardy, temperate varieties should float on the surface, unlike the tropical forms which carry the blooms on clear stalks. If this tendency to lift the flowers clear of the water does arise in hardy water lilies, it should, in most instances, be taken as an indication that the plant is becoming congested and is ready for division. Each stem bears only one flower and, although they all have the familiar star-like overall shape, there is considerable variation in size, degree of doubling and presence of perfume as well, of course, as colour, which ranges from white through yellow to pinks and reds, although there are no blues and purples in the hardy forms. Some varieties change colour markedly as the flower ages. A few garden varieties set seed but the fruit mature below water and are seldom seen.

FOLIAGE Deciduous, circular or more or less oval, mid-green floating leaves, sometimes with rather attractively indented or wavy margins. Variations include various types of variegation and marbling and differing degrees of red-purple anthocyanin pigmentation; that on the undersides is visible only when a strong wind lifts the leaf briefly from the water's surface revealing the colour.

SITE Must have full sun; nothing less will suffice.

PREFERRED WATER DEPTH Varies with variety (see lists) from about 15cm-1m (6in-3ft).

RECOMMENDED POOL SIZE Small to large, depending on the chosen variety.

SPECIAL REQUIREMENTS Must have a sunny situation and varieties must be chosen with care for pool size and depth. Try to avoid planting where they will be constantly splashed by a fountain.

HARDINESS Very hardy, tolerating -20°C (-4°F).

SIZE Varies widely with variety from about 30 x 30cm (12 x 12in) to 2.5 x 2.5m (8 x 8ft) after three or four years.

Nymphaea 'René Gerard'

PLANTING

As rhizomes or plants in spring; in soil in large pools but directly into baskets in smaller ones.

CARE

Little needed once established although dead foliage should be pulled out in autumn. On large, strong plants, this should be done with a certain amount of care for it is all too easy to tug at an apparently moribund leaf only to find that its stalk is still perfectly strong enough to pull up the whole thing by the roots. Dead flower heads should also be removed fairly quickly before they can become waterlogged and sink. Most varieties will benefit from division in spring approximately every three or four years. See also my general comments on water plant care (p.16).

PROPAGATION

By division in spring.

PROBLEMS

Aphids, water lily beetle, leaf miners, fungal leaf spots, rhizome rots and root rots.

RECOMMENDED VARIETIES

Almost all of the water lilies grown in garden pools are hybrids derived from a number of wild, temperate-climate species. Unfortunately, most garden centres stock only a pitifully small range of varieties and so I do recommend strongly that you visit a specialist water plant supplier before making your selection. Don't be tempted, however, by some of the gloriously coloured tropical water lilies that you see at specialist nurseries, many with remarkable blue flowers. They can only be grown in large pools or tanks of water with a temperature that never falls below 10°C (50°F), something that most gardeners are quite incapable of providing.

Because the considerations of vigour, spread and preferred water depth are at least as important as those of colour, I have incorporated this information here instead of listing it separately, as I have done with other types of water plant. In the following lists, I have marked with an asterisk (*) the most widely available varieties.

LARGE WATER LILIES

For water depth 30cm-1m (12in-3ft).
Surface spread up to 1.5m (5ft).
*'Attraction' (rich red with some white streaks, gradually darkening, semi-double, red-brown stamens, green-bronze leaves, magnificent, the best vigorous red); 'Charles de Meurville' (rich red with some white streaks, semi-double, orange-red stamens, deep olive-green leaves with slightly wavy edges); 'Colonel A. J. Welch' (yellow, semi-double, yellow stamens, mid-green, slightly spotted leaves); 'Colossea' (enormous pink flowers, semi-double, yellow stamens, fragrant, green-bronze leaves, markedly hardy and one of the best and most prolific deep-water varieties); 'Gladstoniana' (white, double, fragrant, golden-yellow stamens, dark green leaves, a wonderful plant); 'Gloire du Temple-sur-Lot' (pale pink fading to white, double, yellow stamens, mid-green leaves, shy flowering); 'Mrs Richmond' (pale pink, gradually darkening to red, double, golden-yellow stamens, pale green leaves with slightly wavy edges); *N. alba* (the native British and European water lily, white, double, yellow stamens, reddish leaves, gradually becoming mid-green); *N. tuberosa* 'Richardsonii' (white, semi-double, yellow stamens, pale green leaves, rather shy flowering); *N. t.* 'Rosea' (pale pink, double, red stamens, fragrant, pale green leaves with markedly red-striped stalks).

MODERATELY LARGE WATER LILIES

For water depth 20-60cm (8-24in).
Surface spread up to 1m (3ft).
'Amabilis' (pale pink, single, yellow stamens, deep red to green, markedly pointed leaves); 'Atropurpurea' (deep red, single to semi-double, red stamens with yellow tips, dark red leaves, turning green); 'Caroliniana Nivea' (white, semi-double, yellow stamens, pale green leaves, very pretty, easy and free-flowering); 'Conqueror' (rich crimson with white flecks, semi-double, yellow stamens, purple leaves, gradually turning green); *'Escarboucle' (crimson, semi-double, fragrant, red stamens with yellow tips, red-green leaves turning green, one of the best and most reliable of all water lilies); 'Gonnère' (white, double, golden-yellow stamens, pale green leaves); 'Madame Wilfron Gonnère' (pink, double, golden stamens, mid-green leaves); *'Marliacea Albida' (white, semi-double, golden stamens, dark green leaves, rich purple beneath); *'Marliacea Carnea' (pale pink, gradually darkening, semi-double, yellow-gold stamens, purple leaves, turning dark green, an easy and free-flowering variety); *'Marliacea Chromatella' (yellow, semi-double, golden stamens, dark green leaves with brown spots, shade tolerant); 'Marliacea Rosea' (mid-pink, semi-double, golden stamens, purple leaves, turning dark green); 'Masaniello' (rose-pink, double, orange stamens, dark green leaves); 'Moorei' (pale yellow, semi-double, yellow stamens, dark green leaves with purplish blotches). *N. odorata* (white, single, golden stamens, purple leaves, turning pale green). 'Odorata William B. Shaw' (rose-pink, semi-double, golden stamens, mid-green leaves); 'René Gerard' (reddish-pink, semi-double, yellow stamens, mid-green leaves, bronze-green beneath); 'Sunrise' (deep yellow, semi-double, fragrant, golden-yellow stamens, green leaves with brownish blotches, wavy margins, reddish beneath); 'William Falconer' (deep red, single to semi-double, red stamens with yellow tips, dark purple-red leaves gradually turning green).

WATER PLANTS

Nymphaea Water lily (continued)

RECOMMENDED VARIETIES (CONTINUED)

SMALL WATER LILIES

For water depth 15-45cm (6-18in). Surface spread up to 60cm (24in). 'Albatross' (white, single, golden stamens, dark red leaves, gradually turning dark green); 'Brackleyi Rosea' (rose-pink, gradually fading, semi-double, fragrant, pink stamens, dark green leaves); 'Commanche' (orange-yellow, slowly turning red, semi-double, orange-red stamens, purple leaves, turning green); 'Firecrest' (pink, semi-double, fragrant, orange stamens with red tips, green-purple leaves); 'Gloriosa' (pale crimson, gradually darkening, semi-double, fragrant, red stamens with gold tips, green-bronze leaves); 'Indiana' (pink, turning orange-red, semi-double, yellow stamens, olive-green leaves with darker mottling); *'James Brydon' (deep red-pink, semi-double to double, fragrant, red stamens with gold tips, dark green to purple leaves with reddish flecks, justifiably one of the most famous and popular of all water lilies); *'Odorata Sulphurea Grandiflora' (yellow, semi-double, yellow stamens, mid-green leaves with brownish marbling, pronounced reddish spots beneath); 'Robinsoniana' (orange-red, semi-double, yellow stamens, dark green leaves with darker flecking); 'Rose Arey' (rose-pink, semi-double, fragrant, orange stamens, purple leaves, gradually turning green, a very good and reliable variety); 'Sioux' (yellow, turning orange then rich red, semi-double, yellow stamens, greenish-bronze leaves with brown mottling and rich brown beneath).

VERY SMALL WATER LILIES

For water depth 10-30cm (4-12in). Surface spread up to 30cm (12in). 'Aurora' (yellow, gradually changing through orange to red, semi-double, yellow stamens, mid-green leaves with mottled and marbled patterns); 'Ellisiana' (pale red, gradually darkening, single, yellow stamens, mid-green leaves); *'Froebelii' (vivid red, single, yellow stamens, mid-green leaves); 'Graziella' (coppery-red, single, orange stamens, pale green leaves with purple flecking). *N. tetragona* (syn. 'Pygmaea Alba') (white, single, golden-yellow stamens, dark green leaves, dark red beneath, very tiny indeed, almost the only water lily that can be grown in an aquarium and now naturalized in Britain); 'Laydekeri Fulgens' (crimson, single, red stamens, dark green leaves with purple-brown flecks); 'Laydekeri Lilacea' (lilac-pink, single, yellow stamens, green leaves with sparse brown flecks); 'Laydekeri Purpurata' (crimson, single, orange stamens, mid-green leaves with purple flecks). *N. x helvola* (yellow, single, orange stamens, olive-green leaves). 'Paul Hariot' (yellow, turning reddish-orange, semi-double, fragrant, yellow stamens, mid-green leaves with purplish flecking); 'Solfatare' (yellow, turning orange-yellow and then red, single, yellow stamens, dark green leaves with purple blotches and spots).

Nymphaea 'Froebelii'

Nymphaea x helvola

Nymphaea 'James Brydon'

THE AMAZING MONSIEUR MARLIAC

A number of water lily varieties are prefixed by the name 'Marliacea', a reference to the remarkable French plant breeder, Joseph Bory Latour-Marliac, who raised them around the turn of the century. But a very much greater number of varieties (including many of those that I have recommended) also originated in his nursery at Temple-sur-Lot in the south of France. No other single person has contributed as much to the development of the garden water lily, and it is probable that in no other group of plants has one person's influence been so great. The remarkable thing about M. Marliac, and the reason that relatively little has been achieved since, is that we still have scant idea of how he did it. He used a combination of hardy European and American species to produce his hybrids and was mainly responsible for extending the colour range to more than just the chiefly white-flowered varieties available until that time. But the details of his crosses and selections were imparted to no one and he took his carefully guarded secrets with him when he died in 1911.

Nymphaea 'Conqueror'

WATER PLANTS

Orontium aquaticum Golden club

❝ Yet another member of the arum family and, I think, my favourite of all water plants in its distinctiveness, for it differs from the more familiar aroids in lacking the sheathing, leafy spathe which is reduced in this plant to form a small basal structure. In consequence, the candle-like flower spike is fully and attractively exposed. Orontium is a one-species North American genus that sells on sight if it is seen in flower although its foliage, too, is attractive and appealing. ❞

FLOWERS In late spring, tiny, on white, cylindrical spikes with pronounced golden tips. Small, green fruits form underwater.
FOLIAGE Deciduous, elongated-oval, dark green, silvery above and purplish beneath, partly aerial, floating or submerged, depending on the depth of the water.
SITE Full sun.
PREFERRED WATER DEPTH 10-45cm (4-18in).
RECOMMENDED POOL SIZE Small to large.
SPECIAL REQUIREMENTS Take care not to disturb when well established.
HARDINESS Moderately hardy to hardy, tolerating about -15°C (5°F).
SIZE Will attain spread at water surface of about 60cm (24in) after two or three years.

Orontium aquaticum

PLANTING
As rhizomes or young plants in spring; preferably into planting baskets first.

CARE
Little needed, but dead foliage should be pulled away in autumn. It is best not disturbed once established.

PROPAGATION
By division in spring, or by seeds sown fresh in submerged pots.

PROBLEMS
None.

RECOMMENDED VARIETIES
Normal species only is available.

Polygonum amphibium (syn. Persicaria amphibia) Amphibious bistort, willow grass

"This is a curious plant, a member of the large dock family, the Polygonaceae, a group that contains many pestilential and invasive weeds, and is widely spread throughout the temperate northern hemisphere. But notice its name – amphibium, *not* aquaticum *– it is a species, therefore, that is at home both on land and in water. In its terrestrial habitat, it can be an invasive weed yet, growing in water, it becomes a more docile creature, much less prone to get out of hand and can, indeed, be most attractive. I'm surprised more water plant nurseries don't stock it. "*

FLOWERS In late summer, tiny, neat pink or reddish spikes.
FOLIAGE Deciduous, elongated-oval, mid-green, mostly floating but aerial in shallow water.
SITE Full sun to light shade.
PREFERRED WATER DEPTH Best in 30-45cm (12-18in); in shallower water it becomes invasive.

RECOMMENDED POOL SIZE Medium to large.
SPECIAL REQUIREMENTS Try to restrict to deeper water.
HARDINESS Very hardy, tolerating -20°C (-4°F).
SIZE Will attain spread at water surface of about 60cm (24in) after two or three years.

PLANTING
As young plants in spring; either directly in soil in large pools or, perhaps better, into planting baskets.

CARE
Little needed, but dead foliage may be cut away in autumn if the plant is in fairly shallow water.

RECOMMENDED VARIETIES
Normal species only is available.

PROPAGATION
By division in spring or by seeds sown fresh in damp soil.

PROBLEMS
Aphids, fungal leaf spots.

Polygonum amphibium

WATER PLANTS

Pontederia cordata Pickerel weed

❝I wondered for many years what a pickerel was. Being an angler I really should have known, for it is a local name for various species of pike which, apparently, hide among this plant at the water's edge in its native North American home. The various forms are often listed as marginals but, rather like Polygonum amphibium *(p.49) and* Sparganium *(p.51), they can become invasive and troublesome when grown in this way and I prefer to treat them as deeper water aquatics. I assume and hope that your garden pool doesn't contain pike but, if it is large enough, this is a fine plant to grow for there are very few blue-flowered aquatics, and even fewer that bloom in late summer.❞*

RECOMMENDED VARIETIES
There is a form, *alba*, with white flowers which seems rather to miss the point of the plant; also a variety *lanceolata* with more narrowly elongated leaves and usually darker blue flowers. A plant sometimes listed as *Pontederia azurea* is now more correctly called *Eichornia crassipes* (p.60).

PLANTING
As young plants in spring; directly into the soil in very large pools but otherwise into planting baskets.

CARE
Little care is needed once the plants are fully established, but any dead

FLOWERS In summer until early autumn, tiny, massed in spikes, very pale blue.

FOLIAGE Deciduous, often more or less spear-shaped, glaucous leaves emerging from water.

SITE Full sun.

PREFERRED WATER DEPTH 10-30cm (4-12in) but best and most manageable in a depth of 25-30cm (10-12in).

RECOMMENDED POOL SIZE Medium to large.

SPECIAL REQUIREMENTS Try to avoid planting in shallow water where it will soon become a nuisance.

HARDINESS Very hardy, tolerating -20°C (-4°F).

SIZE Will attain spread at water surface of about 45-50cm (18-20in) after two years.

Pontederia cordata

foliage should be pulled away as autumn approaches.

PROPAGATION
By division of the plants in the spring, or by seeds sown fresh into submerged pots.

PROBLEMS
None.

Sparganium erectum Burr reed

" *Not a reed, although certainly well equipped with burrs, this is another of those plants that behaves itself better when it is moved from the pool edge into deeper water. It's a common* enough British water-side species, but you don't need to be familiar with it in its native habitat for long before its aggressive nature becomes evident. If you have a small pool, avoid it; if you have a *larger one, plant it in deeper water and admire the sharply branched flowering spikes with the small, spherical, prickly flower and fruiting heads that give the species its common name.* "

FLOWERS In summer, small, green, massed in globose, spiky heads; the female flowers are larger and positioned towards the bases of the branched stalks.
FOLIAGE Deciduous or more or less evergreen in milder areas, long, green, rather iris-like leaves.
SITE Full sun to more moderate shade.
PREFERRED WATER DEPTH 10-30cm (4-12in) but best and most manageable in 25-30cm (10-12in).
RECOMMENDED POOL SIZE Medium to large.
SPECIAL REQUIREMENTS Try to avoid planting in shallow water where it will soon become a nuisance.
HARDINESS Very hardy, tolerating -20°C (-4°F).
SIZE Will attain about 1-1.5m x 60cm (3-5ft x 24in) (depending on water depth) after two or three years.

Sparganium erectum

PLANTING
As young plants in spring; directly into the soil in very large pools but otherwise into planting baskets.
CARE
Little needed, but dead stems and foliage should be cut away in autumn.

PROPAGATION
The easiest methods to use are either by division of the plants in spring, or by seeds sown fresh in submerged pots.

PROBLEMS
None.

RECOMMENDED VARIETIES
Normal species only is available.

SUBMERGED PLANTS

Callitriche Water starwort

❝ *Among the more functional, rather than beautiful, oxygenating plants, the various species of* Callitriche *are widespread in their natural distribution throughout Europe and North America but much less common in aquatic plant nurseries. This is rather a pity because it is a plant especially attractive to fish for laying their spawn and it also provides a habitat for minute pond life on which the young fish will feed.* ❞

RECOMMENDED VARIETIES

Callitriche hermaphroditica (syn. *autumnalis*) is the most frequently seen and best species. *C. palustris* (also known as *C. verna*) dies down in winter.

PLANTING

As young plants in spring; in planting baskets in large pools or as weighted clumps sunk into smaller ones.

CARE

None normally needed although this

FLOWERS Insignificant.
FOLIAGE Evergreen, tiny, narrowly elongated and arising in opposite pairs, mid-green, forming rather pretty floating rosettes at the water surface; also some aerial, spear-shaped leaves.
SITE Full sun to very light shade.
PREFERRED WATER DEPTH 10-50cm (4-20in).
RECOMMENDED POOL SIZE Small to large.
SPECIAL REQUIREMENTS None.
HARDINESS Very hardy, tolerating -20°C (-4°F).
SPREAD Indefinite.

is a fairly fast-growing species and will need thinning out every two years.

PROPAGATION

By division in spring or by cuttings, weighted and dropped straight into the water.

PROBLEMS

None.

Callitriche palustris

Ceratophyllum demersum Hornwort

❝ *This is, perhaps, the best oxygenating plant for milder areas with warmer water and, in consequence, slightly less reliable in colder regions. Like many submerged plants, it has an almost worldwide distribution. The common name comes from the spiny edges to the leaves. It is a vigorous plant, and in hot summers, can rapidly choke a small pool entirely with a huge mass of dense, floating vegetation that is very attractive to fish and other pond life but also attractive to blanket weed which will readily grow on, over and through it. It never seems to produce roots and floats both at the surface and in mid-water.* ❞

FLOWERS Insignificant.
FOLIAGE Evergreen in mild areas, but semi-evergreen in colder ones, the plant sinking to the pool bed; tiny, needle-like, green leaves in whorls.
SITE Full sun.
PREFERRED WATER DEPTH 25cm-1.5m (10in-5ft).
RECOMMENDED POOL SIZE Medium to large.
SPECIAL REQUIREMENTS None.
HARDINESS Hardy, tolerating -10 to -15°C (14-5°F).
SPREAD Indefinite.

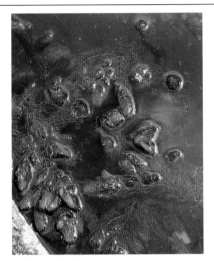

Ceratophyllum demersum

RECOMMENDED VARIETIES
Normal species only is available.

PLANTING
As young plants in spring; simply toss them into the water.

CARE
Must be thinned out at least once a year in all except the largest pools.

PROPAGATION
By breaking off small pieces and dropping them into the water; I can't think of any other plant propagation that is easier.

PROBLEMS
None.

Crassula helmsii

Crassula helmsii (syn. Tillaea recurva)

❝ There's no doubt that some odd things grow on the bottom of ponds and Crassula helmsii *proves the point, as it is almost an aquatic succulent. Yes, it is a real* Crassula, *a native of New Zealand and Australia but widely naturalized in Europe, that creeps along the floor of the pool where no-one notices it, happily oxygenating away, until some of the stems reach the water surface. It is a moderately good oxygenator but is invasive and, as it lacks any honest good looks, it only really merits a place in large pools. ❞*

PLANTING
As young plants in spring, weighted individually and then dropped into the water.

CARE
Should be thinned out every two or three years in all except the largest pools but this is difficult because of

Crassula helmsii

its inaccessibility – another reason for confining it to large pools.

PROPAGATION
Ideally by division in spring but more easily by taking cuttings, weighting them and dropping them straight into the water.

FLOWERS In summer, more or less insignificant, white, growing near the tops of the stems.
FOLIAGE Evergreen, leaves tiny, needle-like and densely packed together on the long, branching stems which are commonly seen floating at the water's surface.
SITE Full sun.
PREFERRED WATER DEPTH 25cm-1m (10in-3ft).
RECOMMENDED POOL SIZE Medium to large.
SPECIAL REQUIREMENTS None.
HARDINESS Fairly hardy, tolerating around -10°C (14°F) but readily surviving cold winters in deep water.
SPREAD Indefinite.

PROBLEMS
None.

RECOMMENDED VARIETIES
Normal species only is available.

SUBMERGED PLANTS

Eleocharis acicularis Spike rush

❝ *Yet again, the ability of nature to mystify and entrance us is manifest in the garden pool because this, for once, is a true rush, a member of the family Cyperaceae, but I have separated it from its fellows (p.108) because it is as a submerged oxygenating aquatic that it is best used in the water garden. Eleocharis acicularis is a common and widespread species throughout Europe and North America and in the wild it is equally happy in the mud at the water's edge.* ❞

Eleocharis acicularis

FLOWERS Only usually formed on plants growing in mud.
FOLIAGE Evergreen, wiry, green-brown, tufted leaves.
SITE Full sun to light shade.
PREFERRED WATER DEPTH Ideally 10-30cm (4-12in) when grown submerged.
RECOMMENDED POOL SIZE Small to large.
SPECIAL REQUIREMENTS None.
HARDINESS Very hardy, tolerating -20°C (-4°F).
SPREAD Height up to about 30cm (12in), depending on water depth; spread on pool floor to about 60cm (24in) in three years.

PLANTING
As young plants in spring; most readily by dropping them individually weighted into the water.
CARE
None normally needed although it

gradually spreads by runners to form an underwater 'lawn', which should be thinned out every few years. Be warned that this is not a task that is easily done while remaining dry.

PROPAGATION
By division in spring.
PROBLEMS
None.

RECOMMENDED VARIETIES
Normal species only is available.

Elodea canadensis

Elodea canadensis Canadian pondweed

❝ *The Canadian pondweed is one of the most mischievous of all pond plants. Not surprisingly, it originated in North America but it was introduced to Europe in the early nineteenth century and very soon blocked rivers, and, at the time, even more importantly, the much-used canals, causing severe obstruction to essential boat traffic. Eventually, the thing quietened down and it is now thought that the original introduction was of a vigorous male clone; the type now sold for water garden use is female and much better behaved. However, it will still need some tending and it is not a plant which should be left to its own devices for long periods.* ❞

RECOMMENDED VARIETIES
Normal species only is available.

SIMILAR SPECIES
The related species, *Elodea callitrichoides* and *E. nuttallii*, require warmer conditions and are better as aquarium plants. Two other common and related species are *E. densa* (now called *Egeria densa*) and *E. crispa* (now called *Lagarosiphon major*) with rather curly leaves which may be grown in pools but, in my experience, they too are much better grown in aquaria.

FLOWERS Sparse, tiny, purple-green at water surface in the summer.
FOLIAGE Deciduous, elongated, fragile bright green leaves in whorls on very long branching stems.
SITE Full sun to light shade.
PREFERRED WATER DEPTH Ideally 10cm-1m (4in-3ft).
RECOMMENDED POOL SIZE Medium to large.
SPECIAL REQUIREMENTS None.
HARDINESS Moderately hardy, tolerating about -5°C (23°F) but surviving cold winters as dormant winter buds.
SPREAD Individual stems reach about 3m (10ft) but the plant forms a large, tangled mass up to 1 x 1m (3 x 3ft) within a year.

PLANTING
As young plants in spring; most readily by dropping them individually weighted into the water.
CARE
Pull it out by the armful every season to avoid it taking over even the largest pool completely.
PROPAGATION
By pulling off pieces in spring, weighting them and dropping them into the water. The plant survives naturally over winter by producing special survival buds that drop into the mud in the autumn.
PROBLEMS
None, although it does seem to me to have a particularly tiresome propensity for attracting blanket weed growth (see pp.20-21).

Fontinalis antipyretica
Water moss, Willow moss

❝I'm sure this must be the only species of moss that gardeners can buy to grow in their gardens, even if it is to be planted underwater. Fontinalis is a true moss with a widespread natural distribution in temperate climates. It is a pretty little thing, forming dark green, feathery tufts that anchor on to submerged stones and sway characteristically in the current of natural streams. I feel it is much better suited to flowing than still water but will, nonetheless, succeed in fairly shallow, clear pools where fish seem to take particular pleasure in spawning in it. ❞

PLANTING
As young plants in spring; ideally, these should be bought already attached to small stones which are ready for dropping in the water but, failing this, the stones may be tied in place with plastic thread.
CARE
None necessary.
PROPAGATION
By breaking up large clumps, ideally with a piece of stone attached.
PROBLEMS
None.

RECOMMENDED VARIETIES
Normal species only is available.

FLOWERS None.
FOLIAGE Evergreen, broadly-elongated, dark green leaves in three rows wrapped tightly along very thin branched stems.
SITE Full sun to more moderate shade.
PREFERRED WATER DEPTH Up to 60cm (24in).
RECOMMENDED POOL SIZE Small to large.
SPECIAL REQUIREMENTS None.
HARDINESS Very hardy, tolerating -20°C (-4°F).
SPREAD Individual stems may reach up to 75cm (30in) but are generally shorter, especially in still water; clumps spread to about 15cm (6in) at the base in three years but the plant splays out from this.

Fontinalis antipyretica

SUBMERGED PLANTS

Lobelia dortmanna Water lobelia

"*Lobelia is a strange genus, and no mistake. Those gardeners used to seeing tender lobelias in hanging baskets will already have been amazed, and I hope entranced, by the almost hardy, rich red-flowered marginal,* Lobelia cardinalis *(p.29); but now we have a genuinely hardy submerged plant in this species from North America and parts of Europe, including Britain. Seen out of flower, it does look purely functional, its hollow stems all but lacking foliage; but when the little nodding pale lilac flowers peep above the water surface in bell-shaped pendants, it combines a certain beauty with its basic oxygenating role.*"

FLOWERS In summer, pendent, bell-shaped, pale lilac, in small inflorescences above the surface of the water.
FOLIAGE Evergreen, elongated dark green leaves in a rosette, from which the almost leafless stems arise.
SITE Full sun to light shade.
PREFERRED WATER DEPTH Ideally 10-60cm (4-24in).
RECOMMENDED POOL SIZE Small to large.
SPECIAL REQUIREMENTS None, although always best in slightly acidic water.
HARDINESS Very hardy, tolerating -20°C (-4°F).
SPREAD Stems extend to about 60cm (24in); spread on pool floor reaches about 30cm (12in) in three years.

PLANTING
As young plants in spring, most readily by dropping them, individually weighted, into the water.

CARE
None needed.

Lobelia dortmanna

PROPAGATION
By division in spring.

PROBLEMS
None.

RECOMMENDED VARIETIES
Normal species only is available.

Myriophyllum Water milfoil

"*Although it may be hard to be over-enthusiastic about any plant that spends its life almost wholly submerged, I think that I would opt for the myriophyllums as my favourite and the most beautiful oxygenators.* Myriophyllum *is a fairly large genus of worldwide distribution and includes some tender species suitable for heated aquaria as well as hardy outdoor aquatics. Its name says it all –* Myriophyllum*, many leaved – although, perhaps rather more accurately, it should be described as 'numerous leaves, greatly divided'.*"

RECOMMENDED VARIETIES
Myriophyllum verticillatum, leaves usually in whorls of five, finely subdivided. *M. spicatum*, leaves usually in whorls of four, more coarsely subdivided. *M. aquaticum*, leaves in whorls of four or five, subdivided but with very short segments.

PLANTING
As young plants in spring; most readily by dropping them, individually, weighted into the water.

CARE
None needed.

PROPAGATION
By cuttings pulled off in the spring and rooted by weighting them into submerged mud.

PROBLEMS
None.

Myriophyllum verticillatum

FLOWERS In summer, minute, pink or yellowish, appearing on long spikes protruding above the water's surface.

FOLIAGE Evergreen, in regular whorls along the stem, usually finely divided to give an overall feathery appearance; where leaves appear on stems above the water surface, they are generally much less divided than those below.

SITE Full sun to light shade.

PREFERRED WATER DEPTH Ideally 10-60cm (4-24in).

RECOMMENDED POOL SIZE Small to large.

SPECIAL REQUIREMENTS None, although *M. verticillatum* and *M. spicatum* are always best in alkaline water.

HARDINESS Very hardy (*M. verticillatum* and *M. spicatum*) tolerating -20°C (-4°F); fairly hardy (*M. aquaticum*) tolerating about -5°C (23°F) but generally surviving colder weather by dying down to a crown in deep water.

SPREAD Varies with species but stems extend to 2-3m (6-10ft); spread on pool floor reaches about 30cm (12in) in three years, and the plant splays out from this.

Myriophyllum aquaticum

SUBMERGED PLANTS

Potamogeton Pondweed

" To a botanist, Potamogeton, *the unenterprisingly named pondweed, is a nightmare of a genus. This is due mainly to the fact that its numerous species vary so greatly under different environmental conditions, that it becomes almost impossible to decide where one ends and another begins. To the water gardener, the species can be limited to two main types, neither very exciting, but functional if given space. They generally die down to overwintering buds. From these new growth arises afresh each spring.* Potamogeton *is a plant for the large pool or lake rather than the small domestic water garden. "*

FLOWERS In summer, small, in greenish-brown spikes emerging above the water.
FOLIAGE Deciduous, entirely submerged, dark green leaves, elongated, strap-like with wavy edges and reminiscent of seaweed in *P. crispus*; narrow and grass-like in *P. pectinatus*.
SITE Full sun to light shade.
PREFERRED WATER DEPTH 10-60cm (4-24in).

RECOMMENDED POOL SIZE Large.
SPECIAL REQUIREMENTS None.
HARDINESS Very hardy, tolerating -20°C (-4°F).
SPREAD Stems extend to 1-2m (3-6ft); spreading over the pool floor these stems reach about 30cm (12in) in three years and the plant growth then emanates out from this.

PLANTING
As young plants in spring.
CARE
Even in large pools, they will require thinning out annually.
PROPAGATION
By division in spring.

PROBLEMS
None.

RECOMMENDED VARIETIES
Potamogeton crispus, wavy leaves.
P. pectinatus, finely divided, rather grass-like leaves.

Potamogeton pectinatus

Ranunculus aquatilis

Ranunculus aquatilis
Water crowfoot

❝ *Several close relatives of the buttercup grace various parts of the water garden but only one, this one, is almost entirely submerged, although I'm never really sure how effective it is as an oxygenator. Like* Potamogeton, *it presents botanists with taxonomic difficulties but is a very much more attractive plant and, given space, its beautiful white buttercup flowers will sit in great profusion on the water's surface.* ❞

PLANTING
As young plants in spring.

CARE
Even in very large pools, it will almost certainly require periodic thinning out if it is not to choke the water completely.

FLOWERS In summer, buttercup-like but pure white with golden centres, floating above the water on short stalks.

FOLIAGE Deciduous, dark green, more or less circular, floating leaves and also very finely divided, grasslike submerged leaves.

SITE Full sun to moderate shade.

PREFERRED WATER DEPTH 10-60cm (4-24in).

PROPAGATION
By division in spring.

PROBLEMS
None.

RECOMMENDED VARIETIES
Normal species only is available.

RECOMMENDED POOL SIZE
Large.

SPECIAL REQUIREMENTS
None.

HARDINESS Very hardy, tolerating -20°C (-4°F).

SPREAD Stems extend to 1.5m (5ft); they spread on the pool floor to about 30cm (12in) in three years, and the plant then splays out from this.

FLOATING PLANTS

Azolla caroliniana Fairy moss

❝*On p.55, I described* Fontinalis, *a plant that I referred to as, probably, the only moss to be grown deliberately as a garden subject. This being the case, where does that leave this delight-ful, fairy-like item of vegetation? As yet another water garden mis-nomer, but also as yet another of water gardening's curiosities for while it is no moss, it is no flower-ing plant either, but the only floating fern in cultivation. Although* Azolla caroliniana *is a native of the warm parts of North America, it survives the British winters very happily because of the small dormant buds that lie in the basal mud.* ❞

PLANTING
As a few fronds, dropped directly into the water.

CARE
Net regularly to limit spread.

PROPAGATION
By simple removal of fronds.

PROBLEMS
None.

FLOWERS None.
FOLIAGE Deciduous, tiny, knobbly green fronds turning rich red in autumn.
SITE Full sun to very light shade.
RECOMMENDED POOL SIZE Small, so that it can be contained by netting. In large pools it will rapidly become out of hand and a nuisance.
SPECIAL REQUIREMENTS Unreliable in moving water.
HARDINESS Barely hardy, tolerating -5°C (23°F) but surviv-ing much colder winters in a dormant state.
SPREAD Will cover about 1sq m (3sq ft) after one year.

RECOMMENDED VARIETIES
Normal species only is available although a few related less hardy species are sometimes offered for aquarium use. *Azolla filiculoides* is sometimes sold for outdoor use but, in my experience, it is less likely to survive cold winters.

Eichornia crassipes Water hyacinth

❝*Eichornia is a real Jekyll and Hyde plant. In its native South American habitat and also in warm, temperate parts of the world, it can be a terrible nui-sance as it multiplies to the extent of severely blocking rivers and other waterways. Indeed, in North America, there are even strict restrictions on its sale for garden use but, in other countries, in small pools in colder areas, where winter temperatures will limit its ambitions, it is a most attrac-tive and valuable floating plant. Its long dangling roots provide fish with convenient spawning places and protection for their young. Its common name is rather appropriate, for the very pretty flowers do indeed closely resemble hyacinth blooms.* ❞

PLANTING
As two or three individual plants, dropped into the water in spring.

CARE
Thin out plants during the summer whenever they threaten to cover the pool. In autumn, pot up a few plants in moist compost in a cool green-house ready to replenish the stock in the pool the following spring.

PROPAGATION
By removal of the young plants on runners at the water's surface.

PROBLEMS
None.

Azolla caroliniana

FLOWERS In summer, bluish-violet, arising above water surface rather like lax hyacinths or even irises.

FOLIAGE Deciduous, curious and appealing, bright green, thick, fleshy leaves with greatly inflated stalks that form floating bladders.

SITE Full sun.

RECOMMENDED POOL SIZE Small to large.

SPECIAL REQUIREMENTS A greenhouse to provide protection for overwintered plants.

HARDINESS Barely hardy, tolerating 0 to -5°C (32-23°F) but stock plants are easily kept over winter.

SPREAD Will cover about 1sq m (3sq ft) within a year.

RECOMMENDED VARIETIES

Normal species only is generally available although sometimes larger flowered and also pink- and yellowish-flowered selections are offered.

Hottonia palustris
Water violet

❝ *Not surprisingly, not a violet; but surprisingly, a member of the primula family. And, perhaps, surprisingly too, a native British plant albeit a rather rare one. It isn't a complete floater, for in shallow water, it will root in the basal mud but, as a pool plant, it is at its best in slightly deeper conditions where it will linger just below the surface for the early part of the summer, and then thrust up a mass of spikes of pale lavender flowers. Look closely (without falling in the water) and you will see why* Hottonia *is a member of the Primulaceae.* ❞

PLANTING
As individual plants, dropped into the water in spring.

CARE
Thin out plants during the summer if they threaten to cover the pool. In

FLOWERS In summer, pale lilac or almost white, in spikes above the water's surface, superficially like those of lady's smock (*Cardamine*).

FOLIAGE Deciduous, in whorls or alternate, mid-green, finely divided and feathery.

SITE Full sun to light shade.

RECOMMENDED POOL SIZE Small to large.

SPECIAL REQUIREMENTS None.

HARDINESS Very hardy, tolerating -20°C (-4°F).

SPREAD Will cover about 1sq m (3sq ft) within a year.

RECOMMENDED VARIETIES

Normal species only is available.

the autumn, it dies down to survive as dormant buds.

PROPAGATION
By removal of young plants or by rooting in wet mud in summer.

PROBLEMS
None.

Eichornia crassipes

Hottonia palustris

FLOATING PLANTS

Hydrocharis morsus-ranae Frogbit

❝ At first sight, the frogbit looks very similar to a baby water lily but closer inspection will also reveal that it is floating rather than rooted, and one can clearly observe that its flowers characteristically have only three petals. It is a native plant of Europe, including Britain, where, if not kept in tight check, it can quickly block up small stagnant pools. However, having said this, it is a pretty thing both in its flowers and foliage and it would be a great shame to exclude it from a garden pool simply because it will need watching and an occasional thinning out before it can become invasive. ❞

FLOWERS In summer, white with yellow centres, three-petalled, rising above the water's surface.

FOLIAGE Deciduous, rounded or kidney-shaped, green-bronze leaves, both floating and raised above the water surface.

SITE Full sun to very light shade.

RECOMMENDED POOL SIZE Small to large.

SPECIAL REQUIREMENTS Always best grown in still, alkaline water.

HARDINESS Very hardy, tolerating -20°C (-4°F) and surviving the winter as dormant buds.

SPREAD Will cover about 1sq m (3sq ft) after one year.

Hydrocharis morsus-ranae

RECOMMENDED VARIETIES
Normal species only is available.

PLANTING
As young plants in spring, simply dropped into the water.

CARE
Thin out the plants occasionally with a net to limit the spread, otherwise blockage of small pools may occur.

PROPAGATION
By careful removal of the young plantlets that form on runners. Produces terminal buds in winter.

PROBLEMS
Snails.

Lemna Duckweed

❝ *Duckweed is one of those plants for which I have always had a soft spot. As a child, perhaps it was because of the pleasure I gained from seeing frogs poking their heads through its light green, all-embracing carpet. Since, I have admired it botanically as one of the smallest of all flowering plants, with each tiny frond or thallus being a complete* individual. *But although duckweeds do sometimes produce flowers, their main method of reproduction is by vegetative division which they achieve with remarkable rapidity, and I must confess that I am more often asked how to remove duckweed from a pool than how to establish it. And the answer is that I don't think it can be removed; so be* warned *and, if you don't want it, it's worth checking other water plants carefully for the presence of contaminating duckweed before introducing them to the pool. In a large pool, however, it is worth bearing in mind that the name, duckweed, does come from the fondness that ducks and other waterfowl have for the plant as their food.* ❞

FLOWERS In summer, flowers uncommon and minute.
FOLIAGE Deciduous, variously shaped, individual minute fronds, each usually producing a single dangling root.
SITE Full sun to light or almost moderate shade.
RECOMMENDED POOL SIZE Small to large.

SPECIAL REQUIREMENTS None, but always best in still or almost still water.
HARDINESS Very hardy, tolerating -20°C (-4°F) and surviving the winter as dormant buds.
SPREAD Will cover about 1sq m (3sq ft) after the first year, but very rapidly covers even large pools thereafter.

RECOMMENDED VARIETIES
Four species are commonly seen, differing in the shape of their fronds: *Lemna minor* (common duckweed) is rounded; *L. trisulca* (ivy-leaved duckweed), is elongated-oval at right angles, forming a star-shape that usually floats just below the surface; *L. gibba*, rounded, swollen; *L. polyrhiza*, rounded with a tuft of roots. The related *Wolffia. arrhiza* is the smallest European flowering plant, rootless and little more than a floating blob of green tissue – hardly the most beautiful thing you've ever seen, but certainly an unusual plant.

PLANTING
As several small plants dropped into the pool in spring.

CARE
Use a net to thin out plants regularly to prevent rapid spreads.

PROPAGATION
By removal of a few fronds.

PROBLEMS
None.

Lemna gibba

FLOATING PLANTS

Stratiotes aloides Water soldier

❝*It will be evident from the entries in this book that the common names of many water plants are, at best, fanciful and, at worst, botanically downright misleading. This one comes into the very fanciful category, for the narrowly pointed leaves are supposed to resemble swords; hence water soldier. In reality, I'm always surprised that it has never been called the water pineapple, as it looks more like a floating pineapple top than anything. In common with one or two other invasive species, its sale is restricted in the United States and other warm areas but it is widely distributed in Europe, including Britain and has a curious habit of rising and sinking in the pool like a yo-yo. It floats just below the surface until mid-summer, then rises, flowers, sinks to the pool bottom and produces peculiar large buds. It then rises to the surface again, the buds develop into young plants, separate from the parent plant and then they sink to the bottom until the spring when, yes, you've guessed it, they rise again to the surface.* ❞

FLOWERS In summer, small, white and usually rather hidden among the foliage.
FOLIAGE More or less evergreen with a stiff rosette of toothed, rather narrowly elongated leaves.
SITE Full sun to light shade.
RECOMMENDED POOL SIZE Small to large.
SPECIAL REQUIREMENTS Always prefers still, alkaline water and is best cultivated in water at least 30cm (12in) deep to allow the plants to sink out of harm's way.
HARDINESS Very hardy, tolerating -20°C (-4°F).
SPREAD Will cover about 1 sq m (3 sq ft) after one year.

RECOMMENDED VARIETIES
Normal species only is available.

PLANTING
As young plants in spring, dropped into the water.
CARE
Thin out plants occasionally with a net to limit spread.
PROPAGATION
By removal of the young plants that develop in spring.
PROBLEMS
None.

Stratiotes aloides

Trapa natans Water chestnut

❝*Yes, this is the water chestnut found so commonly in Chinese restaurants. The large thorny fruit is the edible part of the plant, but don't be tempted to nibble any that may be growing in your pool as* Trapa natans *is poisonous when raw. In reality, it is strictly a rooted aquatic but the leaf rosettes, which arise on long stems, appear to be floating free. It is yet another plant that has restrictions placed on its sale in warm countries, for it can cause severe blockages in waterways but in Britain this is unlikely to become a problem because of the cooler climate. The plant is certainly unlike much else in the pool, with its rosettes of peculiar leaves and their very unusual inflated stalks.* ❞

PLANTING
As young plants in spring, dropped into the water or as fruits (see under propagation).
CARE
Thin out plants occasionally in order to limit spread.
PROPAGATION
By the large spiny fruits which will germinate in the pool mud in spring and give rise to a stem from which the floating leaves develop.
PROBLEMS
None.

RECOMMENDED VARIETIES
Normal species only is available.

Trapa natans

FLOWERS In summer, small, white and well hidden among the foliage.
FOLIAGE Deciduous, annual, with a floating rosette of rather angular, toothed leaves, each on an inflated stalk.
SITE Full sun to light shade.
RECOMMENDED POOL SIZE Small to large.
SPECIAL REQUIREMENTS Always best in almost still, slightly acidic water, preferably at least 30cm (12in) deep. See also comments under hardiness (below).
HARDINESS Barely hardy, tolerating about -5°C (23°F) and although it will survive winters as the fruits in a dormant state, unfortunately, I find that these are not produced consistently and it is only after warm summers that they may be relied upon. At other times, the plant must be treated as an annual and renewed each year, or possibly a few stock plants overwintered in tanks in a warm greenhouse.
SPREAD Will cover about 1sq m (3sq ft) after one year.

Utricularia vulgaris Bladderwort

❝ Even by water garden standards, this is an odd thing, a submerged, floating rootless plant that looks like a mass of green threads covered with tiny pimples. It rises to the surface in summer to thrust flowers that look like tiny orange snapdragons up out of the water. It then sinks again and continues its carnivorous habit, trapping minute aquatic creatures and consuming them. It survives the winter, when light and food are scarce, as dormant buds. ❞

Utricularia vulgaris

FLOWERS In summer, small, gold-orange, rising above the water's surface and looking like small antirrhinums.
FOLIAGE Deciduous, dark green, tangled hair-like mass of submerged, floating leaves.
SITE Full sun to light shade.
RECOMMENDED POOL SIZE Small to large.
SPECIAL REQUIREMENTS Always best in almost still, slightly acidic water.
HARDINESS Very hardy, tolerating -20°C (-4°F) as dormant buds.
SPREAD Will cover about 50sq cm (20sq in) after about one year.

PLANTING
As young plants in spring, dropped into the water.

CARE
Thin out plants occasionally to limit the spread.

PROPAGATION
By division in spring.

PROBLEMS
None.

RECOMMENDED VARIETIES
A large number of superficially very similar species is available, especially from specialist suppliers. However, you must be sure that any plants that you buy are described as hardy, as some are for aquarium use only. *Utricularia vulgaris* is the commonest and most reliable.

BOG PLANTS

Alchemilla mollis Lady's Mantle

❝ It has become a habit among gardening writers to extol the virtues of Alchemilla *by making reference to the drops of water that collect on the leaves 'like little beads of mercury'. It is an apt simile that is just a part of the appeal of this delightful ground cover plant. It suffers only one drawback in that it is deciduous and dies back in autumn to an unattractive hump but, for me, the lime green, ribbed leaves and the feathery flowers in summer are more than adequate compensation. At the edge of a bog garden, it is essential. ❞*

CARE
Mulch in autumn and early spring. Give a balanced general fertilizer in spring, cut back flower heads as they turn brown and fade, and cut all foliage right back to the crown in the late autumn.

PROPAGATION
By division in autumn or spring.

PROBLEMS
None.

RECOMMENDED VARIETIES
The normal species that will be seen most frequently is *Alchemilla mollis* although the related, similar but less vigorous *A. alpina* is a better choice for smaller gardens. *A. conjuncta* has very pretty, rather star-shaped leaves, is less invasive, less shade tolerant, and is suitable for the drier edge of the bog garden.

SITE Light to moderate shade, ideally with dappled light.
PREFERRED SOIL Most, except very heavy, cold soils; light to moderate moisture.
HARDINESS Very hardy, tolerating -20°C (-4°F).
SIZE Will attain about 50 x 50cm (20 x 20in) after three or four years; *A. alpina* around half of this.

Anaphilis margaritacea Pearly everlasting

❝ Not, perhaps, the most obvious choice for a bog garden as it is only moderately tolerant of wet soils, but I find it grows well and looks most attractive at the margins where plants with small white flowers are rather at a premium. In many respects, it is a typical member of one major group of the daisy family, with its rather flat flower heads (its relationship to yarrow is very evident) and elongated, greyish-silver leaves – a colour that is at a premium in the bog garden. The flowers dry well for attractive indoor arrangements. ❞

CARE
Mulch in autumn and early spring. Give a balanced fertilizer in spring, cut flower heads as they fade in autumn and cut the foliage back to soil level.

Alchemilla mollis

SITE Full sun to light shade.
PREFERRED SOIL Most except very heavy cold soils; light moisture.
HARDINESS Very hardy, tolerating -20°C (-4°F).
SPREAD Will attain 30-45 x 30-45cm (12-18 x 12-18in) each year once established.

RECOMMENDED VARIETIES
The variety *Anaphilis margaritacea cinnamomea* has very dense wool beneath the leaves. 'Neuschnee' has supposedly much better and whiter flowers.

PROPAGATION
By division in autumn or spring.

PROBLEMS
None.

Ajuga reptans Bugle

❝ *Why the name bugle? I don't know and I'm not sure that anyone else does either but ajugas are valuable, if never spectacular, plants for bog garden ground cover. All forms are a little rampant and can overwhelm a small garden but, given adequate room, their shade tolerance makes them particularly effective when they are planted beneath taller species. Their only real drawback is that* they are not always seen clearly enough, for the best varieties have very dark coloured foliage and this doesn't help in the shade. Yet planted in full sun, where their colours would be most evident, they sulk and never do well. The typically lipped flowers that betray their place in the family Labiatae range from purple to light blue, with only one white variety. ❞

SITE Moderate to deep shade.
PREFERRED SOIL Most; moderate moisture.
HARDINESS Very hardy, tolerating -20°C (-4°F).
SIZE Will attain about 15cm x 1m (6in x 3ft) after about three or four years.

CARE
Mulch in the spring and the autumn for as long as is practical until well established. Give a balanced general fertilizer in spring. In smaller gardens, they are best trimmed back in autumn; in wilder areas may be left untended. Divide every three or four years if they threaten to get out of hand.

RECOMMENDED VARIETIES
Ajuga reptans 'Alba', with white flowers; 'Atropurpurea' has the richest bronze-purple leaf colour of all the varieties; 'Burgundy Glow' has deep wine-red leaves but these can fade rather unattractively; 'Multicolor' (which is also called 'Rainbow') is true to its name with shades of yellow, pink and red on a bronze leaf but I don't much care for it; 'Variegata' has cream edges on very dark green leaves.

SIMILAR SPECIES
Ajuga pyramidalis is just one of a number of related but far less invasive species.

PROPAGATION
By division in spring.

PROBLEMS
Mildew.

Anaphilis margaritacea

Ajuga reptans

BOG PLANTS

Artemisia lactiflora

❝ *In most gardens, artemisias are grown for their soft feathery, silvery-grey foliage, but when a plant is called* lactiflora *it suggests that there is something special about its flowers too. And indeed there is, for this Chinese species has a mass of tiny flowers borne through the summer on tall plume-like stems. It is an imposing plant for a mixed planting although, because of its size, it is ideally placed towards the back. I find it best when not crowded in the way that bog garden species so often are, for the soft foliage is prone to disfiguring grey mould in the damp atmosphere. It is, paradoxically, a plant for wet soil but less for wet air.* **❞**

CARE

Mulch in spring and autumn. Give a balanced general fertilizer in spring. It

SITE Full sun.
PREFERRED SOIL Most; light to moderate moisture.
HARDINESS Very hardy, tolerating -20°C (-4°F).
SIZE Will attain about 1.5m x 60cm (5ft x 24in) in approximately two years.

RECOMMENDED VARIETIES

Selected forms with variegated or otherwise coloured foliage are occasionally seen but have no special merit.

will probably require staking. Cut down dead top growth in late autumn. Divide every three or four years to avoid overcrowding.

PROPAGATION

By division in autumn or spring.

PROBLEMS

Mildew, grey mould when the plants are overcrowded.

Artemisia lactiflora

Aruncus dioicus
Goat's beard

❝ *It is pure alphabetical chance that brings* Aruncus *close to* Artemisia lactiflora *for the plants are totally unrelated, yet, in general appearance, rather similar. The tall, feathery flower heads of* Aruncus *really are most unexpected for a plant in the family Rosaceae, but tall they certainly are and the goat's beard (there's a stupid name for you) is one of the few plants that could, indeed, be planted behind the artemisia and still be visible.* **❞**

CARE

Mulch in spring and autumn. Give a balanced general fertilizer in spring. Despite the height, the plants have stout stems and should not require staking. Cut down dead top growth in late autumn. Divide every three or four years.

PROPAGATION

By division in autumn or spring, or by seed sown in summer or early autumn in a humus-rich, soil-based compost in a cold-frame.

PROBLEMS

None.

SITE Light to moderate shade.
PREFERRED SOIL Most, provided there is good organic content; light to moderate moisture.
HARDINESS Hardy, tolerating -15 to -20°C (5 to -4°F).
SIZE Will attain up to 2 x 1m (6 x 3ft), 'Kneiffii' less than half of this.

Aruncus dioicus

RECOMMENDED VARIETIES

The normal species is the best, but for smaller gardens there is a shorter variety called 'Kneiffii'.

Arum italicum

❝ *A good water garden should be full of arums of one sort or another, although most of them grow either in the water or at its very edge. I tend to grow this one in the relatively less sodden soil of the bog garden where it always seems to thrive, and the fact that it is fairly often seen in normal, moist herbaceous borders is testimony to its preference for these slightly drier conditions. In all respects, it is typical of the temperate-climate aroids. This is demonstrated in its greenish spathe with white interior, its yellow spike of minute flowers and the striking red fruits that follow, the latter proving particularly favourable fodder to slugs. However Arum italicum scores most notably in having a quite beautiful variant which has very pretty marbled foliage.* ❞

CARE

Mulch in spring and autumn if practicable. Also give a balanced general fertilizer in spring and disturb as little as possible once established.

PROPAGATION

By division in spring, or by seed washed from ripe fruits collected in autumn and sown in a humus-rich, soil-based compost maintained at about 20°C (68°F).

PROBLEMS

Slugs will tend to eat the red fruits but are seldom troublesome on the foliage itself.

SITE Moderate to deep shade.
PREFERRED SOIL Humus-rich; light to moderate moisture.
HARDINESS Fairly to moderately hardy, tolerating -10 to -15°C (14-5°F).
SIZE Will attain 25-30 x 20-30cm (10-12 x 8-12in) after three years.

RECOMMENDED VARIETIES

Easily the best form and the one always to choose is 'Pictum' (sometimes called var. *marmoratum* or var. *italicum*) which has leaves in which the dark green is marbled with cream.

Arum italicum 'Pictum'

BOG PLANTS

Astilbe

I'm sorry, but I can't bring myself to like these plants, yet I know I am in the minority by the frequency with which I find myself having to issue this apology. The feathery form and the colour of astilbes (in particular those luminous pinks) might, just about, be acceptable in a modern, formal garden setting but in the semi-natural environment of a wilder bog garden, they just aren't for me. Interestingly and unexpectedly, they belong to the saxifrage family and they hybridize with much abandon, as can be seen from the huge range of varieties now available. 99

CARE
Mulch in spring and autumn and give a balanced general fertilizer in spring. The top growth may be cut down after the flowers fade or may be left but the plants will not require staking. Divide occasionally; every five or six years should suffice.

SITE Light to moderate shade, seldom as successful in full sun.
PREFERRED SOIL Organic, light to moderate moisture.
HARDINESS Very hardy, tolerating -20°C (-4°F).
SIZE Varies with variety. There are some dwarf forms but most common types are in the range 50 x 30cm (20 x 12in) to 1.5m x 60cm (5ft x 24in).

RECOMMENDED VARIETIES
As I have indicated, there are swarms of hybrid varieties in colours ranging from white through various degrees of shocking pink to red. You will also find a considerable spread in flowering time and height but the range of varieties differs from nursery to nursery. If I was pressed to grow an astilbe, I think it would be one of the whites such as 'Snowdrift'.

PROPAGATION
By division in spring.

PROBLEMS
None.

Bergenia
Elephant's ears

Bergenias epitomize the functional, rather than the evidently beautiful, among garden plants; their function is to smother the soil in shady places with their large, fleshy leaves, whether in the wet, shady parts of a bog garden or the drier shade of a conventional border. I'm only just convinced that they merit a place in smaller water gardens but the forms with the dark reddish-coloured leaves and deep red flowers might justify it. 99

SITE Light to deep shade; they will grow in full sun but never look their best.
PREFERRED SOIL Almost any, including heavy clays, moderate moisture.
HARDINESS Very hardy, tolerating -20°C (-4°F).
SIZE Will attain about 30-45 x 30-45cm (12-18 x 12-18in) after three years.

CARE
Mulch in spring and autumn and give a light dressing of a balanced general fertilizer in spring. Cut down the old flower spikes as they fade; the foliage is evergreen.

PROPAGATION
By division in autumn or spring, although this may prove to be quite difficult where the plant has formed large, old and woody clumps.

PROBLEMS
None.

Astilbe hybrids

Several species are available through specialist suppliers but the best all-round bog garden plants are *Bergenia cordifolia* 'Purpurea', with rich purple leaves and deep pink flowers and the hybrid 'Bressingham Ruby', rather similar but with very choice dark red flowers. 'Bressingham White' is, perhaps, the most appealing of the remainder with bright green leaves and white flowers.

Bergenia cordifolia 'Purpurea'

Brunnera macrophylla

❝ I have grown few plants that differ so much as Brunnera *in appearance when grown in good rather than poor soils. At their best, brunneras have an appeal that is almost a combination of forget-me-nots and omphalodes (they are all members of the Boraginaceae family). In floral terms, they couldn't be much prettier, but the foliage tends to be their weak point; something else they share with others in the family and they suffer particularly when neglected. ❞*

CARE

Mulch in spring and autumn and give a light dressing of a balanced general fertilizer in spring. Cut back the old flower spikes and trim back foliage as it browns.

PROPAGATION

By division in autumn or spring, by root cuttings, preferably taken in early spring or, with some forms, by seed sown in spring in a humus-rich, soil-based compost.

PROBLEMS

Leaf-attacking insects and pests.

SITE Light to deep shade; they will grow in full sun but, in my experience, always suffer from it.
PREFERRED SOIL Fairly rich, organic, light to moderate moisture.
HARDINESS Very hardy, tolerating -20°C (-4°F) but browned by cold winds in exposed sites.
SIZE Will attain about 40 x 60cm (16 x 24in) after two or three years.

'Dawson's White' has a green and white leaf variegation; 'Hadspen Cream' has leaves with cream edges; 'Langtrees' has green leaves with white blotches.

Brunnera macrophylla

BOG PLANTS

Campanula lactiflora

"I love campanulas but the taller ones can be hard work for they will flop and so, ideally, should be staked. Yet, as I have already pointed out, staking a plant in a bog garden, even at the edges where campanulas are most successful, can be a pretty messy exercise. You can avoid it, how-ever, by close planting and sur-rounding the campanulas with other, slightly more robust species. There are considerable differences in height between the varieties and the shorter, stiffer ones are more suitable for water garden plantings. "

CARE
Mulch in spring and autumn and give a balanced general fertilizer in spring. Cut back dead flower stems if possible and trim back dead foliage as neces-sary. Divide the plants every three or four years.

SITE Light to moderate shade, will be reasonably successful in full sun.
PREFERRED SOIL Organic, but not acidic site, light to mod-erate moisture.
HARDINESS Very hardy, tolerating -20°C (-4°F).
SIZE Will attain about 80-90 x 60cm (32-35 x 24in) after three years.

RECOMMENDED VARIETIES
In a bog garden, I generally pre-fer to see the white 'Alba' with its luminous flowers which create contrast, but other colours are available if they take your fancy: pink in 'Loddon Anna' and a pur-plish-blue in 'Pritchard's Variety'.

PROPAGATION
By division in autumn or spring.
PROBLEMS
Slugs will attack young shoots.

Campanula lactiflora 'Alba'

Cimicifuga

"To describe slender, white-flowered plants as candle-like is understandable but there are few for which the simile is more appropriate than the North American and Asian cimicifugas. In reality, their fragile appear-ance is deceptive for they are tough with firm, wiry stems. I always think of them as being among those garden plants that look better en masse and also when seen at a distance, when those flower spikes take on a quite ethereal appearance. "

SITE Light to moderate shade, ideally dappled; not truly reliable in full sun.
PREFERRED SOIL Rich, organic, prefers light to moder-ate moisture.
HARDINESS Very hardy, tolerating -20°C (-4°F).
SIZE About 2-2.5m x 60-75cm (6-8ft x 24-30in) within three or four years.

CARE
Mulch in spring and autumn and give a balanced general fertilizer in spring. Cut back dead flower stems once blooming is over. Divide every three or four years.
PROPAGATION
By division in autumn or spring. Some forms come true from seed sown in a soil-based compost in late summer in a cold-frame.
PROBLEMS
None.

RECOMMENDED VARIETIES

RECOMMENDED VARIETIES

Cimicifuga racemosa has divided leaves, lovely in both the normal green-leaved species and the purple-leaved 'Purpurea'. *C. simplex* (sometimes called *C. ramosa*) has more or less entire leaves which are also at their most attractive in the purple-leaved 'Atropurpurea'.

Cimicifuga racemosa

Dicentra formosa Bleeding heart

❝ *I confess that I had never thought of dicentras, or bleeding hearts, as water garden plants until a few years ago, when I first realized how they suffer from drought. They wilt and look extremely unhappy. Since then, I have always grown them in rich, wet conditions. But they are, nonetheless, difficult to place, for those pink and white dangling flowers don't blend readily with many other plants, and certainly not with anything yellow.* **❞**

CARE
Mulch in spring and autumn and give a balanced general fertilizer in spring. Cut back flower stems after blooming. Do not disturb once established.

PROPAGATION
Most readily done from seed in summer in a soil-based compost in a propagator at a minimum temperature of 15°C (60°F).

PROBLEMS
None.

RECOMMENDED VARIETIES
The normal species, *Dicentra spectablis* and *D. formosa* have predominantly pink flowers and, in view of my remarks above, you might prefer the white-flowered variants of each, both called *alba*. There are also several hybrids, among which 'Pearl Drops' is one of the best and most attractive whites.

Dicentra formosa alba

SITE Light to moderate shade, ideally dappled; I think they are less successful in full sun.
PREFERRED SOIL Deep, rich, organic, prefers light to moderate moisture.
HARDINESS Very hardy, tolerating -20°C (-4°F).
SIZE The true species will attain about 45-60 x 45-60cm (18-24 x 18-24in); the hybrids reach about half this.

BOG PLANTS

Dodecatheon Shooting stars

❝*There is an ancient derivation for this very classical-sounding name, as* Dodecatheon *means 'twelve gods' in Greek, but I have no idea why these delightful rhizomatous flowers should be associated with gods of any number. They are classically lovely with their swept-back petals and prominent anthers. Unexpectedly, perhaps, they are members of the primula family and one or two species are sometimes known as American cowslips. They must have moisture but after flowering in the spring, they fade and pass into dormancy with the coming of the summer sun.* ❞

SITE Light and preferably dappled shade.
PREFERRED SOIL
Moderately organic, not clay, prefers light moisture.
HARDINESS Very hardy, tolerating -20°C (-4°F).
SIZE Varies with species from about 20-50 x 15-25cm (8-20 x 6-10in) after four or five years.

RECOMMENDED VARIETIES
The commonest species is *Dodecatheon meadia* with rich purple flowers (white in f. *album*) but among others seen frequently are D. *dentatum* (white), D. *hendersonii* (purple) and D. *pulchellum* (mauve-purple, or large and red in the striking variety 'Red Wings').

CARE
Mulch in the spring and then again in the autumn. Also give a balanced general fertilizer in the spring. Allow the foliage to die back naturally and then try to disturb the plant as little as possible once it has become fully established.
PROPAGATION
By division in the spring (although the best results are achieved by removing parts of the plant from the periphery of a large clump without disturbing either the body or the root system). Alternatively, by seed sown fresh in the early summer in a moist, soil-based compost which is kept in a shaded cold-frame.
PROBLEMS
None.

Dodecatheon meadia

Eupatorium

❝*The native European* Eupatorium cannabinum, *hemp agrimony, is one of the plants of my childhood for it was my riverside companion on boyhood fishing trips. Despite its common name, the plant is not related to the true hemp and does not yield cannabis. It is a wonderful plant for attracting bees and butterflies to the bog garden with its mass of feathery flowers that, only on very close inspection, reveal it as belonging to the daisy family, the Compositae. It is, by no means, a grand thing but it is a fine plant for informal places.* ❞

Eupatorium cannabinum

CARE

Mulch in the spring and the autumn and then give a balanced general fertilizer in the early spring. Cut down any dead growth right back to the soil level in late autumn after the foliage begins to die back.

PROPAGATION

By division in the spring or alternatively by seed sown in the autumn in a moist soil-based compost protected in a cold-frame.

PROBLEMS

None.

SITE Full sun or light shade.
PREFERRED SOIL Most soil types, including moderately heavy, prefers light to more moderate moisture.
HARDINESS Very hardy, tolerating -20°C (-4°F).
SIZE *E. cannabinum* will attain a height of about 1.5m x 60cm (5ft x 24in) and *E. maculatum* will grow to slightly more than half this after approximately three or four years.

RECOMMENDED VARIETIES

Eupatorium cannabinum is the species that will be seen most frequently, although its double-flowered variant 'Flore Pleno' is well worth looking out for. Not all other species are suitable for moist soils, but perhaps the best of those that are is the lower-growing, North American *E. maculatum*, especially in its form 'Atropurpureum', which has large, deep purple flowers.

Euphorbia palustris

❝ As gardeners begin to acquire experience, Euphorbia *is one of the genera that they come to appreciate for its all-round value in the herbaceous border. There are, however, relatively few species suitable for really wet soils but I think this European plant is the best of them. It bears rather flat and most impressive yellow and green flower heads, typical of the herbaceous euphorbias, but it is a big plant and certainly not one for rather more modest water gardens. ❞*

SITE Full sun or light or almost moderate shade.
PREFERRED SOIL Rich, fairly organic, with light to moderate moisture.
HARDINESS Very hardy, tolerating -20°C (-4°F).
SIZE Will attain up to 1m x 80-90cm (3ft x 32-34in) after three years.

CARE

Mulch in spring and autumn and give a balanced general fertilizer in spring. Cut down dead growth to soil level in late autumn but not before the attractive yellowish foliage tints have been appreciated.

PROPAGATION

I think this is probably easiest carried out by softwood cuttings taken in early summer although it will also come true from seed sown fresh in a soil-based compost in a cold-frame. Division can be rather risky because the cut roots may rot.

PROBLEMS

None.

RECOMMENDED VARIETIES

Normal species only is available.

Euphorbia palustris

BOG PLANTS

Filipendula Meadowsweet

❝ *The very name 'meadow-sweet' is redolent of lush meadows in high summer, the hum of insects and fragrance drifting from countless floral nectaries. And this aptly describes the natural habitat of this tall and lovely plant, which is quite indispensable for all except the very smallest bog gardens. The flowers are tiny and the flower heads feathery, not at all what most gardeners expect from the rose family, and although some of the pink shades are assertive, the creamy whites are a delight.* ❞

Filipendula ulmaria 'Aurea'

SITE Full sun to light or more moderate shade.
PREFERRED SOIL Organic, rich, moderate moisture.
HARDINESS Very hardy, tolerating -20°C (-4°F).
SIZE F. rubra and F. ulmaria are the largest species, attaining about 2 x 1m (6 x 3ft) in three years; some forms are smaller and F. palmata and F. purpurea are about half this size.

RECOMMENDED VARIETIES
The native European *Filipendula ulmaria* is the most frequently seen, the golden-foliaged 'Aurea' and the double-flowered 'Flore Pleno' being particularly striking. The pink-flowered 'Rosea' I find less attractive. Among other species commonly available are the Asian F. palmata with palm-shaped leaves and pink or red flowers, according to variety, and two other pink-flowered types, the North American F. rubra and the oriental F. purpurea.

CARE
Mulch in spring and autumn and give a balanced general fertilizer in spring. Cut down dead flower stems and foliage in autumn. The stems are tough and shouldn't need staking.

PROPAGATION
By division in autumn or spring, or from seed, preferably sown fresh in the autumn in a soil-based compost and kept in a propagator at around 12-15°C (53-59°F).

PROBLEMS
Generally none although aphids may be troublesome.

Fritillaria meleagris Snakeshead

❝ *The genus* Fritillaria *is one of those in which the species are fairly familiar, but are so different from each other that the fact that they are related comes as a considerable surprise. The more familiar of the two common species is the Asian crown imperial,* Fritillaria imperialis, *but this is a plant for the more conventional border. The bog garden plant is the much smaller European* F. meleagris, *with the most endearing, nodding, bell-like spring flowers in various shades of purple and also white, with varying degrees of chequer patterning. They are perfect for growing among damp grass.* ❞

CARE
Give a balanced general fertilizer in spring and do not disturb once they are fully established.

PROPAGATION
By removing and replanting small bulbs or bulbils, or from seed, sown fresh in summer in a soil-based compost in a sheltered cold-frame.

PROBLEMS
None.

RECOMMENDED VARIETIES
The normal species generally has purple flowers with a slightly paler chequered pattern and the commonest of the selected forms is the white-flowered *alba*.

SITE Light to moderate shade although it will grow in full sun if it is sheltered among some other vegetation.
PREFERRED SOIL Organic, rich, moderate moisture, tolerant of high alkalinity.
HARDINESS Very hardy, tolerating -20°C (-4°F).
SIZE Will attain about 25-30cm (10-12in) in height, and spreads to about 15cm (6in) from a single bulb after three or four years.

Fritillaria meleagris

Gentiana Gentian

❝ *Pretty well every gardener knows a gentian, although rather fewer grow them. Fewer still grow them well and hardly any grow them in a water garden. Yet while there certainly are species that require well drained or even* *dry hillsides and mountains, there are one or two choice ones for wetter places. The slender-leaved and slender-stemmed willow gentian is one; the slender and appropriately named marsh gentian is the other.* ❞

SITE Full sun to light to moderate shade.
PREFERRED SOIL Organic, rich, moderate moisture, must be acidic for *G. pneumonanthe*, and preferably acidic for *G. asclepiadea*.
HARDINESS Very hardy, tolerating -20°C (-4°F).
SIZE The arching flowers stems of *G. asclepiadea* will attain about 60cm (24in), the more upright ones of *G. pneumonanthe* about half this, and they spread to about 25cm (10in) in four years.

CARE
Mulch in spring and autumn and give a balanced general fertilizer in spring.

RECOMMENDED VARIETIES
Gentiana asclepiadea (willow gentian), flowers blue (or white in the form *alba*) on long stems.
G. pneumonanthe (marsh gentian) short stems with a terminal cluster of deep blue flowers.

Disturb as little as possible once the plant is established.

PROPAGATION
By softwood cuttings taken in summer and rooted in a fairly rich, soil-based compost in a covered cold-frame or a propagator with slight bottom heat. Also fairly readily grown from seed sown in early spring in soil-based compost then kept in a propagator at about 20°C (68°F).

Gentiana pneumonanthe

PROBLEMS
None.

BOG PLANTS

Geranium phaeum

❝ I bore friends and acquaintances alike with my devotion to the genus Geranium *as I don't believe that any garden can be complete without a fair selection of its wonderful species. In the bog garden, however, there is only one that I grow with confidence but, fortunately, it is one of my firm favourites: the deep, deep purple-flowered* Geranium phaeum. *If a dark-flowered plant can be said to light up a dark and heavily shaded water garden, then I would say that this is quite definitely it. ❞*

RECOMMENDED VARIETIES
The normal species is the one to choose; the white-flowered 'Album' is inferior and does not even look like the same species.

CARE
Mulch in spring and autumn and give a balanced general fertilizer in spring. Cut down dead flower stems in spring and a smaller second flush of flowers will follow in autumn. Cut down to just above the crown in late autumn. Divide every three or four years. Does not need staking.

PROPAGATION
By division in autumn or spring.

PROBLEMS
None.

SITE Light to deep shade.
PREFERRED SOIL Tolerates most but best and most luxuriant in deep rich, organic soils; moderate moisture.
HARDINESS Very hardy, tolerating -20°C (-4°F).
SIZE Will attain 60 x 60cm (24 x 24in) in three years.

Geranium phaeum

Geum rivale Water Avens

❝ A number of geums are woodland plants and a good many are plants of damp woodlands too. I have picked out just one as being particularly useful in the bog garden for it enjoys even wetter conditions than most. It is a fairly common British native plant – the appropriately named water avens – but it also exists in quite a considerable number of excellent cultivated variants which display a wide collection of different colours. ❞

Geum rivale 'Leonard's Variety'

RECOMMENDED VARIETIES
The normal species has purple flowers but among the other selected forms are 'Leonard's Variety' (pinkish-orange) and 'Lionel Cox' (yellowish-orange).

CARE
Mulch in spring and autumn and give a balanced general fertilizer in spring. Cut down dead flower stems in summer and cut down foliage to soil level in late autumn. Divide every three or four years. Does not need staking.

PROPAGATION

By division in the autumn or spring; although geums may be raised easily from seed, the best forms do not come true.

PROBLEMS

Leaf feeding insect larvae such as sawflies and leaf miners.

SITE Light to moderate shade.
PREFERRED SOIL Tolerates most, but best in deep rich, organic soils; light to more moderate moisture.
HARDINESS Very hardy, tolerating -20°C (-4°F).
SIZE Will attain about 30 x 20cm (12 x 8in) in about three or four years.

Gunnera manicata

❝ *You need a very big water garden to grow a gunnera; but if you do have a very big water garden, this is a plant that you cannot do without. It's often referred to as the giant rhubarb, but no rhubarb was ever this spectacular. Gunnera and rhubarb are not even related but the leaves are similar in shape if not in size, those of the South American gunnera being up to 2m (6ft) in diameter. The flower spike is not exactly pretty but is certainly pretty impressive, massed with small greenish-red flowers, 1.5m (5ft) or more in height and extremely stout. Plant a gunnera in your bog garden and flocks of ducks will shelter beneath it.* ❞

Gunnera manicata

SITE Full sun to moderate shade but with shelter from cold winds and late frosts.
PREFERRED SOIL Tolerates most but best in deep, rich, organic soils, with moderate to high moisture.
HARDINESS Fairly hardy to moderately hardy, tolerating -10 to -15°C (14 to 5°F).
SIZE Will attain 2 x 1.5m (6 x 5ft) after three or four years.

CARE

Mulch in spring and autumn and give a balanced general fertilizer in spring. Cut the dead flower stems right down

---

RECOMMENDED VARIETIES

The species normally seen is *Gunnera manicata* but *G. tinctoria* is also fairly common and is rather more compact.

---

in summer after flowering is complete and cut down foliage in late autumn, using it to cover the crown and provide protection from winter frosts.

PROPAGATION

By division in the spring and also from seed sown fresh in the autumn in a soil-based compost in a sheltered cold-frame.

PROBLEMS

None.

BOG PLANTS

Heloniopsis orientalis

❝ Very few gardeners would know a heloniopsis if they tripped over one which is a pity for it is a truly lovely but uncommon oriental, liliaceous, rhizomatous plant for the bog garden. In spring, the nodding and rather spidery heads of pinkish-mauve flowers hang above a rosette of fresh, evergreen foliage that looks a delight in front of taller things. ❞

SITE Light to moderate shade; shelter from cold winds.
PREFERRED SOIL Best in leaf mould-rich, organic soils; light to moderate moisture.
HARDINESS Moderately hardy, tolerating about -10°C (14°F).
SIZE Will attain 30 x 15cm (12 x 6in) in about three years.

CARE
Mulch lightly in spring and autumn and give a balanced general fertilizer in spring. Dead flower heads may be cut down or left but the foliage is evergreen and should not be cut back. Leave undisturbed once established.

PROPAGATION
By division in spring (although this will disturb the clumps), or by seed sown fresh in a soil-based compost and then kept in a cold-frame.

PROBLEMS
None.

RECOMMENDED VARIETIES
The normal species is the only one available.

Heloniopsis orientalis

Hemerocallis
Day lily

❝ Day lilies are fairly aptly named. The individual flowers don't last for much more than a day (although more do continue to appear over many weeks) and they are true, rhizome-forming members of the lily family. They have become increasingly popular in recent years as border perennials with the introduction of many more varieties, but they still haven't received the recognition they deserve as bog garden plants. The individual trumpet-shaped flowers are now offered in a wide range of colours including both some lovely reds and some pretty dreadful oranges. Some are most pleasingly fragrant. ❞

Hemerocallis 'Pink Damask'

SITE Full sun to light shade.
PREFERRED SOIL
Hemerocallis tolerate most soils but are always best in fairly rich loams; light moisture.
HARDINESS Very hardy, tolerating -20°C (-4°F).
SIZE Varies with variety but generally will attain 75cm-1m x 60cm (30in-3ft x 24in) after three years.

CARE

Mulch in the spring and the autumn and give a balanced general fertilizer in the spring. Cut back any dead flower stalks and cut foliage right back to the soil level as it will shrivel in autumn. Divide every two years; some of the older forms are invasive and their ambitions must be curtailed if gardeners are to keep them properly under control.

PROPAGATION

By division in autumn or spring.

PROBLEMS

None.

RECOMMENDED VARIETIES

There are now many tens of varieties, but unfortunately most of these are only obtainable from a fairly restricted range of nurseries. Among the best of those that I have found to be more widely available are 'Anzac' (rich red), 'Black Magic' (very dark purple), 'Burning Daylight' (strong, rich orange), 'Catherine Woodbery' (pink, green and white), 'Hyperion' (yellow), 'Stella de Oro' (shorter than most and golden-yellow).

Hosta
Plantain lily

"Hostas have become among the most familiar garden plants in recent years, thanks largely to the huge range of new varieties, many of them raised in the United States. They have always been thought of as subjects for the wetter and shadier parts of the garden although they are now recognized as much more versatile and will tolerate drier and sunnier places too. Their foliage is pretty, and their flowers are just about good enough, but their common role as slug fodder will always limit their total acceptance by the gardening fraternity. "

Hosta undulata marginata

CARE

Mulch in spring and autumn and give a balanced general fertilizer in spring.

SITE Full sun to moderate shade.
PREFERRED SOIL Hostas tolerate most soils but are always best in fairly rich loams; light to moderate moisture.
HARDINESS Very hardy, tolerating -20°C (-4°F).
SIZE Varies with variety from about 30 x 30cm-1m x 60cm (12 x 12in-3ft x 24in) after about four years.

RECOMMENDED VARIETIES

From the enormous range of varieties, I can only recommend those that I have experience of growing, but have to add that I have been less than impressed by those claimed to be slug tolerant. *Hosta* 'Blue Moon', ribbed, bluish leaves; *H. decorata*, ribbed leaves, white-cream edges; *H. fortunei*, bluish-green, or yellow with green streaks in the form *albopicta*; *H.* 'Francee', green leaves with white edge; *H.* 'Ginkgo Craig', green with white edges; *H. lancifolia*, green, narrowly-elongated leaves; *H. undulata marginata* (also called 'Thomas Hogg'), green with cream edge is, I think, my favourite, an opinion that I seem to share with a great many slugs).

Cut back dead flower stalks promptly and cut or pull away dead foliage as soon as it starts to become frayed and tattered in autumn.

PROPAGATION

By division in autumn or spring.

PROBLEMS

Slugs and snails.

BOG PLANTS

Iris

❝ *I've already extolled the virtues of irises in general, and now it's the turn of those that are best in the damp soil of the bog garden. Again, the instantly recognizable iris flower is their common identifying feature, but the four rhizomatous species that I think the best here come from widely separated parts of the world.* Iris innominata *is a more or less evergreen species from North America;* I. sibirica, *the so-called Siberian iris is, in fact, from a wide area of Europe and Asia;* I. orientalis *is a misnomer as it originates in Eastern Europe; while* I. chrysographes *is from China and Burma.* **❞**

SITE Full sun.
PREFERRED SOIL
Moderately rich, moderately organic, light moisture.
HARDINESS Very hardy, tolerating -20°C (-4°F).
SIZE Varies with species; *I. sibirica* and *I. orientalis* reach about 50-90 x 30cm (20-34 x 12in) after three years, *I. chrysographes* about two-thirds and *I. innominata* about one-third of this.

Iris sibirica

Iris chrysographes

CARE

Mulch in spring and autumn and give a balanced general fertilizer in spring. Dead flower heads should be cut down as far as the first sheathing leaf. Where cold weather has caused the foliage to die back, it should be trimmed in late autumn, but where it survives in a more or less evergreen state, it should be left. Divide approximately every three or four years after flowering is completed.

PROPAGATION

By division after flowering in early summer, re-using only the fresh parts of the rhizome at the periphery of the clump and planting them directly at the soil surface, rather than burying them deeply.

PROBLEMS

Aphids, snails, rhizome-rotting fungi, fungal leaf spots.

RECOMMENDED VARIETIES

Iris chrysographes, in the normal species, has dark red-purple flowers with gold marks; good selected varieties include the so-called 'black form' which, not surprisingly, is very, very dark purple, and several others with names such as 'Black Knight' that serve to indicate that selection in this species has almost invariably been for the darkest colours.
I. innominata is usually offered only in the normal species, but the colour varies enormously from creamy-white through yellow to orange, brownish, pink and purple; do make sure that you buy plants in flower so you can select those that particularly take your fancy. *I. orientalis*, (sometimes called *I. sanguinea*) is available only in the normal species and is dark reddish-purple with white markings.
I. sibirica is available in the normal species only and is a dark bluish-purple in colour.

In addition to this varied list, a number of hybrids have been developed from one or more of these species and, among these, the best suited to the bog garden are 'Caesar's Brother' (whoever thinks up these extraordinary names?), dark purple; 'Ego', blue; 'Helen Astor', dark purple and red with white markings; 'Mrs Rowe', soft pink; 'Papillon', pale blue; 'Sparkling Rose', mauve-pink with blue markings; 'Tropic Night', dark blue-purple; 'Wisley White', white.

Leucojum
Snowflake

It's many years since I first discovered leucojums and now I don't know how I or anyone else could garden without them. They have much in common with snow-drops but are taller and later flowering. Indeed, I often think that it is the later flowering habit that has led to their relative un-familiarity. Producing the first flowers at the beginning of the year guarantees the popularity of real snowdrops, but there are many more garish blooms around by the time that leucojums take over. They have a special appeal that should not be ignored and, while they will grow in moist bor-ders, they are also valuable at the drier edge of the bog garden.

CARE

Mulch in the spring and the autumn and, in addition to this, give a balanced

SITE Light to moderate shade.
PREFERRED SOIL Rich, deep and organic, light moisture.
HARDINESS Hardy, tolerating about -15 to -20°C (5 to -4°F).
SIZE Up to 20 x 10cm (8 x 4in) after two or three years; half as much again for 'Gravetye Giant'.

RECOMMENDED VARIETIES

Only the normal species of the winter flowering *Leucojum vernu-mis* is available, but easily the best form of the spring flowering *L. aestivum* is 'Gravetye Giant'.

general fertilizer or bone meal in spring. Cut off dead heads after flow-ering is complete.

PROPAGATION

By division approximately every four or five years after flowering while the plant is still in full leaf, or by sowing fresh seed in a soil-based compost at about 20°C (68°F).

PROBLEMS

None.

Leucojum aestivum

BOG PLANTS

Lychnis chalcedonica Catchfly

❝Catchflies do catch the odd aphid or two on their felty-sticky leaves, although their efforts seem to do little to reduce the overall insect population in the neighbourhood. But no matter, for they are pretty if never spectacular plants for a mixed planting. While some of them require well drained and relatively dry places, this eastern European species, sometimes called the Maltese cross, is a good plant for moister areas, including the front and margins of the bog garden. It is a plant familiar in old cottage gardens where its flame-red flower heads never seem too assertive. In the water garden, it needs placing carefully if it isn't to clash. ❞*

SITE Full sun to light shade.
PREFERRED SOIL
Moderately rich, moderately organic, light moisture.
HARDINESS Very hardy, tolerating -20°C (-4°F).
SIZE Will attain about 1m x 40cm (3ft x 16in) after three or four years, *L. flos-cuculi* and *L. x haageana* about two-thirds the height of this.

CARE
Mulch in spring and autumn and give a balanced general fertilizer in spring. Cut down dead flower heads and cut down all top growth in late autumn. Divide every three or four years.

RECOMMENDED VARIETIES
In addition to the normal species, a white form, 'Alba' and a double-flowered variety, 'Flore Pleno', are often seen. Related species that will also thrive in wet soils are *Lychnis flos-cuculi*, the red-flowered native ragged robin and the bright orange-red-flowered hybrid *L. x haageana*.

PROPAGATION
By division in spring or autumn, or by seed preferably sown fresh in late autumn in a soil-based compost in a propagator at about 20°C (68°F).
PROBLEMS
None.

Lychnis chalcedonica

Lysichiton Skunk cabbage

❝Lysichitons are the bog garden plants par excellence*; provided your bog garden is pretty large. They are aroids, as their very large and obvious spathes will reveal in spring, and the yellow of* Lysichiton americanus *is particularly evident and assertive, making its presence apparent from metres away. After flowering, when the huge leaves emerge, they could easily be mistaken for some monstrous* Bergenia *of elephantine proportions. Examined at close quarters, the heavy aroma produced by the foliage will immediately explain the origin of the common name. ❞*

SITE Full sun to light or a more moderate shade.
PREFERRED SOIL Preferably rich, organic, moderate to high moisture.
HARDINESS Hardy, tolerating about -15°C (5°F).
SIZE Will attain about 75 x 60cm (30 x 24in) after three or four years.

CARE
Mulch in spring and autumn and give a balanced general fertilizer in spring. Cut down dead top growth in late autumn and, in milder areas, pack bracken or similar protective covering over the crowns for the winter. Do not disturb once established.
PROPAGATION
By careful removal of young off-sets

Lysichiton camtschatcense

from the base of established plants, or by removal of self-sown seedlings (hybrids may result where the two species are grown together). If mature clumps are disturbed, they may stop flowering for several seasons. It may also be raised from seed, sown fresh in summer in soil-based compost and kept permanently wet in a fairly well sheltered spot.

PROBLEMS

None.

RECOMMENDED VARIETIES

Lysichiton americanus, yellow spathe; *L. camtschatcense*, white spathe.

Lysimachia Loosestrife

❝ *An interesting name, loosestrife, said to originate from the use of the plants to ward off flies from around working horses in summer and thus lessen or 'loosen' the strife between them. The plants are interesting and much underrated, especially* Lysimachia punctata *which will grow almost anywhere, even in fairly dry soil although I think I have seen it more in wet places. By contrast, the native* L. nummularia, *the prostrate creeping Jenny, is very much a plant of streamsides while* L. nemorum, *the yellow pimpernel is found typically in damp woodlands.* ❞

CARE

Mulch *L. punctata* in spring and autumn (the other two species are too low-growing to mulch satisfactorily) and give a balanced general fertilizer in spring. Cut down dead top growth of *L. punctata* in late autumn. All are best left undisturbed to spread *ad lib.*

SITE Light to moderate shade.
PREFERRED SOIL Preferably rich, organic, with light to moderate moisture for *L. punctata*, much higher moisture for the other two.
HARDINESS Very hardy, tolerating -20°C (-4°F).
SIZE *L. punctata* will attain about 90cm-1.2m x 45-60cm (34in-4ft x 18-24in) after three or four years, *L. nemorum* and *L. nummularia* about 5 x 30-40cm (2 x 12-16in).

PROPAGATION

By division in spring or autumn, by softwood cuttings of *L. nummularia* in early summer, rooted in a soil-based compost which is kept moist in a sheltered spot; also by seed sown fresh in a soil-based compost in a cold-frame.

PROBLEMS

None.

RECOMMENDED VARIETIES

Normal species only are available apart from *L. nummularia* which is best in the golden-foliaged variant, 'Aurea'.

Lysimachia nummularia 'Aurea'

BOG PLANTS

Lythrum salicaria Purple loosestrife

❝ *By another of those alphabetical coincidences, one loosestrife is followed by the other, although they are quite unrelated; the yellow* Lysimachia *is related to the primula while* Lythrum, *with its tall, slender spikes of tiny purple flowers is the true loosestrife with its own family, the* Lythraceae. *It's also another of those plants that, for me, conjures up river banks and fishing trips and I consider it indispensable for the wilder water garden. In reality, it will grow in most border soils, but the bog garden is its spiritual home.* ❞

SITE Full sun to light shade.
PREFERRED SOIL
Moderately rich, moderately organic, light to moderate moisture.
HARDINESS Very hardy, tolerating -20°C (-4°F).
SIZE Will attain about 1m x 45cm (3ft x 18in) after three or four years.

CARE
Mulch in spring and autumn and give a balanced general fertilizer in spring. Cut down dead flower heads and cut down all top growth in late autumn. Divide every three or four years.

PROPAGATION
By division in spring or autumn, or by seed (not of selected, named varieties) preferably sown fresh in late autumn in a soil-based compost in a cold-frame. They can also be propagated from softwood or Irishman's cuttings taken in spring and rooted in a soil-based compost in a cold-frame.

PROBLEMS
None.

Lythrum salicaria

Parochetus communis

❝ *I've included this interesting and lovely member of the pea family for those gardeners with smaller bog gardens in mild areas. It is seen most frequently among alpine collections, for it is naturally a plant of high, moist meadows in parts of tropical Africa and Asia. Its tropical origins needn't concern you unduly for high altitudes in the tropics can be pretty cool and, if you have the right conditions, I would experiment with it. I love it for its blue flowers, so unusual on a plant with the leaves and growth habit of a clover.* ❞

SITE Light shade.
PREFERRED SOIL Preferably organic, with light to moderate moisture.
HARDINESS Fairly hardy, tolerating about -5°C (23°F).
SIZE Attains about 5 x 25cm (2 x 10in) after three years.

CARE
Give a light dressing of bonemeal in spring and then leave undisturbed once established.

PROPAGATION
By removal of the naturally rooted runners.

PROBLEMS
None.

RECOMMENDED VARIETIES
Normal species only is likely to be available.

Parochetus communis

Peltiphyllum peltatum (syn. Darmera peltata)

Peltiphyllum peltatum (syn. Darmera peltata) Umbrella plant

❝ This is by no means the only species to be known as the umbrella plant but it is without a doubt the most striking. It is a North American member of the saxifrage family and is a very good plant for stream banks as well as more conventional bog gardens. The foliage is large and lush but it is the flower heads that will arouse most interest in spring before the leaves have begun to emerge. The flowers are small, white or pink, and formed in rather flat inflorescences on top of woolly stems. ❞

CARE
Mulch in spring and in autumn, give a dressing of general fertilizer in spring, cut down dead flower stalks and cut back dead foliage in autumn.

PROPAGATION
Most easily propagated by dividing the plant in spring.

PROBLEMS
None.

SITE Full sun to fairly moderate shade.

PREFERRED SOIL Preferably organic, moderate to quite high moisture.

HARDINESS Hardy, tolerating -15 to -20°C (5 to -4°F).

SIZE Will attain about 1-1.2m x 60-75cm (3-4ft x 24-30in) after three years, 'Nana' perhaps half this height.

RECOMMENDED VARIETIES
The normal species is the choice for larger gardens but in limited space the smaller but otherwise similar 'Nana' is a better bet.

BOG PLANTS

Persicaria

❝As far as the majority of gardening books are concerned, for Polygonum, you must read Persicaria since most species have been re-categorized from one genus to the other. They aren't exciting plants, I am sure most people would agree, but they do have a certain individuality with their neat, compact, massed spikes of tiny flowers. The fact that some native species are rather noxious weeds shouldn't put you off growing their relatives, although the vicious pink colour and rather graceless way of dying down in autumn just might. Some species require rather dry or at least well drained conditions, but those that I have chosen have performed well for me in wetter places. ❞

Persicaria amplexicaulis

SITE Full sun to light shade.
PREFERRED SOIL Will tolerate most except very heavy sites, light to an almost moderate moisture.
HARDINESS Very hardy, tolerating -20°C (-4°F).
SIZE Varies with species from about 30 x 30cm (12 x 12in) after three or four years for *P. millettii* to 1.2m x 75-85cm (4ft x 30-34in) for *P. amplexicaulis*.

RECOMMENDED VARIETIES

Persicaria amplexicaulis 'Atrosanguinea', very deep red; var. *pendula* (also called 'Arun Gem'), bright pink, pendulous flowers, unusual. *P. campanulata*, pale pink; 'Alba', white, very pretty; *P. millettii*, rich red.

CARE

Mulch in the spring and autumn, at least until well established, and give a balanced general fertilizer in the spring. Cut down any dead flower heads after blooming and cut down all top growth in late autumn. Divide every three or four years.

PROPAGATION

By division in spring or autumn.

PROBLEMS

None.

Phormium
New Zealand flax

❝New Zealand, because that is where phormiums originate, and flax because the tough leaf fibres have been used for making cloth and containers. Most are large, evergreen, clump-forming plants, very evidently related to agaves, but the best forms have variegated foliage, are somewhat tender and should be positioned in sheltered spots. Although not demanding of bog garden conditions, they do require moist soil and are particularly useful because most plants with this type of stiff, sword-like foliage and habit need rather drier conditions for growth. ❞

Phormium 'Rainbow Surprise'

SITE Full sun to light shade.
PREFERRED SOIL Rich, moderately organic, fairly light moisture.
HARDINESS Fairly to moderately hardy, tolerating -5 to about -15°C (23-5°F), the hybrids and variegated forms being significantly less hardy than the species.
SIZE Varies enormously from about 30 x 25cm (12 x 10in) after three or four years for the very dwarf hybrids to 4.5 x 1m (15 x 3ft) for *P. tenax*, so check label descriptions carefully if you want to avoid embarrassment.

RECOMMENDED VARIETIES
Phormium tenax, the normal species, has stiff, upright, dark green leaves, usually with reddish edges, but among good selected forms are 'Purpureum' (dark purple leaves) and 'Nanum Purpureum' (dwarf form, also with purple leaves).
P. cookianum has a more drooping habit with green leaves which usually bear a pink or greenish flush. There are several hybrids, most derived from this species. Among the best are the 'Maori' series, which come in wonderfully varying degrees of very pretty red, pink, orange and yellow leaf variegation, 'Sundowner' with purple, predominantly cream-edged leaves but with other coloured streaks too, and the 'Rainbow Surprise' which also exist in a wide range of colours. But do remember, they are more tender.

CARE
Mulch in spring and autumn and give a balanced general fertilizer in spring. Cut down dead flower heads and cut away dead and browned foliage in spring, but be careful not to cut down the top growth completely as it is evergreen. The more tender forms will probably benefit from having a layer of bracken or some other protective material packed around the crowns in winter. Do not divide once it is fully established unless necessary for propagation.
PROPAGATION
By careful division in spring, or by removal of off-sets from the base.
PROBLEMS
None.

Physostegia virginiana Obedient plant

❝ *An old but fairly indolent gardening friend once said that something called an obedient plant would be just up his street: a species that did exactly as it is told, always flowered to order, never became out of hand and grew with the minimum amount of attention. Sadly, I had to disillusion him because the curious name for this rather typical labiate comes from the fact that if the flowers are turned by hand, they stay where they are put. But well-behaved or not, this is an attractive perennial with spikes that are truly packed with flowers in late summer.* ❞

CARE
Mulch in spring and autumn and give a balanced general fertilizer in spring. Cut down dead flower heads after blooming and top growth in late autumn. Divide every three years.
PROPAGATION
By division in spring or autumn.
PROBLEMS
None.

SITE Full sun to light shade.
PREFERRED SOIL Will tolerate most except very heavy sites, light moisture.
HARDINESS Very hardy, tolerating -20°C (-4°F).
SIZE Most forms will attain about 75-90 x 45-60cm (30-35 x 18-24in) after three or four years, although 'Vivid' reaches a height of only about 50 x 30cm (20 x 12in).

RECOMMENDED VARIETIES
'Alba', white; 'Crown of Snow', white; 'Bouquet Rose', mauve-pink; 'Summer Snow', white; 'Vivid', deep pink, lower-growing.

Physostegia virginiana

BOG PLANTS

Potentilla palustris **Marsh cinquefoil**

Earlier, I mentioned a distinction between geums and their close relatives, the potentillas, in that the former generally prefer wetter places and the latter almost entirely dry ones. But this plant is an exception, a striking, dark-flowered native species of Potentilla *for the bog garden. It is slowly but not aggressively invasive and I find that its flower colour makes it a good companion for the many yellow-flowered bog garden plants.*

CARE
Mulch in the spring and autumn, and give a balanced general fertilizer in spring. In wilder gardens, the dead flower heads are best left to self-seed but they may be cut back to give a tidier appearance. Divide every three or four years.

PROPAGATION
By division in spring or autumn but also, and most easily, by removal of rooted runners.

PROBLEMS
None.

SITE Full sun to moderate shade.
PREFERRED SOIL Acidic, not rich, moderately organic, moderate to almost high moisture.
HARDINESS Very hardy, tolerating -20°C (-4°F).
SIZE Will attain about 30-45 x 30-45cm (12-18 x 12-18in) after two or three years.

RECOMMENDED VARIETIES
Normal species only is available.

Potentilla palustris

Primula

I am far from alone in thinking that Primula *is one of the most important genera in the entire garden. Indeed, many gardeners would put it at the top of the list; although, to be fair, some of them would be alpine rather than water gardeners. Such is the scope of the primulas that there are species indispensable for the bog garden, while others are essential for the alpine trough or the woodland glade. I have selected those that I have found most successful but there are plenty of others. The ones listed here range in size, in form and in colour although their requirements and cultivation are fairly similar. Whatever bog garden plants you grow, there can be absolutely no doubt that there must be some primulas among them.*

SITE Full sun to moderate shade.
PREFERRED SOIL Fairly rich, organic, preferably slightly acidic, light or almost high moisture.
HARDINESS Very hardy, tolerating -20°C (-4°F).
SIZE Variable, see Recommended Varieties.

Primula pulverulenta

RECOMMENDED VARIETIES

Primula alpicola, heads of bell-shaped, variable, yellow, purple or white flowers on graceful 20-30cm (8-12in) tall stems. Some named colour selections are available. *P. denticulata* (drumstick primula), spherical heads of small mauve flowers atop 30cm (12in) tall stems in spring, numerous colour selections, most notably *alba*, white and 'Inshriach Carmine', deep red; others are given *ad hoc* but, at least, descriptive names such as "ruby", "red", "lilac" or "purple". *P. florindae* (Himalayan cowslip), superb, like a 75-80cm (30-32in) tall cowslip with shaggy, yellow flower heads in early summer: a few selected colour forms ("orange", "yellow", and so forth), are offered. *P. rosea*, neat 10-20cm (4-8in) tall stems of variously shaded pink flowers in early summer. The most notable selected form is 'Grandiflora' (not surprisingly, a plant with larger flowers).

Candelabra primulas are a large group of species and hybrids in varying heights but sharing the distinctive and beautiful habit of bearing the flowers in whorled series on the stems. Among the many that I recommend are *P. pulverulenta*, 90cm (36in), pale pink or mauve flowers; *P. beesiana*, 60cm (24in), deep red with yellow centres; *P.* x *bulleesiana* (including Asthore Hybrids), 60cm (24in), a wide range of colours including yellow, orange, pink, red and purple; *P. bulleyana*, 75cm (30in), deep orange; *P. burmanica*, 60cm (24in), red-purple with marked yellow eye; *P. chungensis*, 60cm (24in), orange with red centres; *P. cockburniana*, 20-30cm (8-12in), rich orange, one of my real favourites, but sadly a rather short-lived perennial; *P. helodoxa*, 75cm (30in), yellow; *P. Inshriach.* Hybrids (including *P.* 'Inverewe'), 50cm (20in), orange-pink, a beautiful but, rather sadly, sterile example, and *P. japonica*, 75cm (30in), pink.

CARE

Mulch lightly in spring and autumn (although this is difficult with the smaller species and unnecessary with those in the wettest spots), and give a balanced general fertilizer in spring. Leave dead flower heads until seed has been dispersed and then cut back where feasible. Divide every three or four years.

PROPAGATION

By division in spring or autumn, or by seed sown fresh on the surface of a humus-enriched, soil-based potting compost in a shaded spot where the temperature will not exceed 20°C (68°F). Some hybrids and selections will not come true from seed and, for most, germination is slow and erratic.

PROBLEMS

Slugs and snails, leaf miners, fungal leaf spots, viruses.

Primula florindae

BOG PLANTS

Pulmonaria Lungwort

❝ *Pulmonarias won't be in most people's list of bog garden plants but they are in mine, simply because I became so frustrated with them looking miserable in a well drained spot in my own garden that I moved them to the edge of the bog garden, and was very pleased that I did. The name lungwort refers to the spotted appearance of the leaves (rather like lung tissue) and to an old belief that the plants were, therefore, of value in treating lung complaints. The ground-covering foliage does little more than set off the delightful spring flowers, which are a lovely bright blue in the best forms but, as with so many other blue-flowered plants, fading to red.* ❞

SITE Light to moderate shade.
PREFERRED SOIL Most, providing it is rich and fertile and preferably organic, light to moderate moisture.
HARDINESS Very hardy, tolerating -20°C (-4°F).
SIZE Will attain 15-25 x 30-45cm (6-10 x 12-18in) after four years.

CARE
Mulch in autumn and also, if possible, in spring before the new leaf growth commences; give a balanced general fertilizer in spring. In wilder gardens, the dead flower heads are best left to self-seed but they may be cut back to give a tidier appearance. Divide every three or four years.

PROPAGATION
By division in spring or autumn.

PROBLEMS
None.

RECOMMENDED VARIETIES
Pulmonaria angustifolia is the earliest-flowering form and Gertrude Jekyll's plant 'Munstead Blue' is the best colour; *P. longifolia*, with elongated leaves is best in the deep purple form 'Bertram Anderson'; *P.* 'Mawson's Blue' is the finest blue of all, while Vita Sackville-West's version, *P. officinalis* 'Sissinghurst White' is a white, if that is what you want.

Rheum Ornamental rhubarb

❝ *While* Gunnera *(p.79) is often incorrectly called an ornamental rhubarb, this plant really is one. It isn't as big as the gunneras but it needs plenty of room. Depending on variety, both leaves and flower heads can contribute to the overall attractiveness. Choose varieties carefully, not only for their potential size, but also because some are appreciably less hardy than others.* ❞

Pulmonaria officinalis

R. palmatum 'Atrosanguineum'

SITE Full sun to light or moderate shade.
PREFERRED SOIL Most, provided rich, organic and fertile. Intolerant of heavy soils. Light to almost moderate moisture.
HARDINESS Hardy, tolerating about -15°C (5°F).
SIZE Will attain 1.2-1.5m (4-5ft) (or up to 2m (6ft) for *R. palmatum*) x 1-1.5m (3-5ft) after three or four years.

RECOMMENDED VARIETIES

Rheum palmatum, rich reddish-purple leaves, white flowers; 'Atrosanguineum', reddish flush throughout the entire plant; *rubrum*, rich pink flower spikes; *R.* 'Ace of hearts', leaves rich red beneath, flowers pink.

CARE

Mulch in autumn and spring and mound deep mulch protection over the crown in winter. Give a balanced general fertilizer in spring. The large flower heads are best left after flowering and the whole top growth cut down later as it deteriorates. Divide every three or four years.

PROPAGATION

By division in spring although, with large plants, the massive crown may be difficult to cut and a sharp spade or axe may be needed.

PROBLEMS

Crown rot if grown in cold, waterlogged positions.

Rodgersia

This really is a strange plant: the leaves, at least of the commonest species, which are so similar to those of the horse-chestnut, are produced not on a tree but on a majestic perennial, and a member, odd to relate, of the saxifrage family. The majesty of the plant is enhanced when the spikes of tiny, usually white flowers appear in summer. It is one of those plants that really looks at home by a woodland stream but like a fish out of water situated anywhere else.

CARE

Mulch in autumn and spring at least until well established and give a balanced general fertilizer in spring. Leave the flower heads in place after flowering because reddish seedheads develop later in the season. Best left undisturbed once fully established.

PROPAGATION

By division in spring, or alternatively by seed sown fresh in late summer in

Rodgersia aesculifolia

a humus-enriched, soil-based compost in the shelter of a cold-frame during the cold spells of winter.

PROBLEMS

None.

SITE Moderate to deep shade.
PREFERRED SOIL Rich, organic, light to almost moderate moisture.
HARDINESS Hardy, tolerating about -15°C (5°F).
SIZE Varies with each species from about 1m x 45cm (3ft x 18in) for *R. podophylla* to around 1.5m x 60cm (5ft x 24in) for *R. aesculifolia*.

RECOMMENDED VARIETIES

The normal species to be offered is *Rodgersia aesculifolia* with the horse-chestnut-like leaves, but among other very good plants are *R. pinnata*, deeply-divided leaves, white flowers, 'Elegans' is the best white-flowered form with 'Superba' a pink-flowered variant; *R. podophylla*, palm-shaped leaves; and *R. sambucifolia* (for a change, leaves not like a horse-chestnut but an elder), white flowers.

BOG PLANTS

Saururus cernuus
Lizard's tail, Swamp lily

❝ *This North American oddity can just about be grown as a marginal plant with its roots in the 'swamp', although I prefer to have it in the bog garden where the fresh green, heart-shaped leaves create a very fresh-looking ground cover. The rather fluffy, tail-like heads of creamy flowers droop most appealingly above the leaves in summer. The only other common genus in this family is the multi-coloured* Houttuynia, *a plant whose foliage is as brash as this one's is subtle.* **❞**

RECOMMENDED VARIETIES
Normal species only is available.

CARE
Mulch in autumn and spring and give a balanced general fertilizer in spring. Cut down dead foliage in autumn.

PROPAGATION
By division in spring.

PROBLEMS
None.

SITE Moderate shade.
PREFERRED SOIL Preferably organic and fairly rich, moderate to high moisture.
HARDINESS Hardy to very hardy, tolerating -15 to -20°C (5 to -4°F).
SIZE Will attain 25-30 x 25-30cm (10-12 x 10-12in) after three or four years.

Saururus cernuus

Saxifraga fortunei

❝ *Although I have included one or two unexpected members of the saxifrage family in the book, this one is a true member of the genus* Saxifraga. *As a whole, this is a group still thought of as alpine, but while the majority of species are most at home in an alpine garden, several border perennials and also this one – a fairly low-growing plant with pretty rosettes of dark-coloured, rounded leaves and sprays comprising masses of tiny star-like flowers in autumn – are suitable for the damp garden.* **❞**

CARE
Mulch in spring and in autumn, covering the crowns after the foliage has died down to give protection over winter (although in mild areas, it may be at least partially evergreen). Give a balanced general fertilizer in spring. Once fully established, it is best left undisturbed.

PROPAGATION
By division in spring.

PROBLEMS
None.

SITE Light to moderate shade.
PREFERRED SOIL Most, but preferably rich and fertile, light to almost moderate moisture.
HARDINESS Hardy, tolerating about -15°C (5°F).
SIZE 25-35 x 25-30cm (10-14 x 10-14in) after three years.

The normal species is widely available although a number of hybrids derived from it are frequently seen. Among the best are 'Rubrifolia', with reddish leaves, and 'Wada', with rich red leaves, a superb plant; several of the hybrids have Japanese names, for the parent is a Japanese species and very popular in Japan as a garden plant.

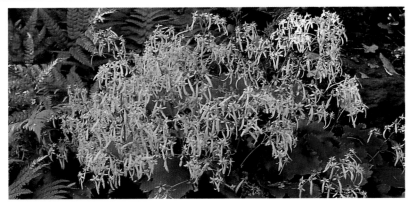

Saxifraga fortunei

Schizostylis coccinea Kaffir lily

" *I would be the last person to pretend that* Schizostylis *is a bog garden exclusive for, these days, it is much more likely to be seen as a normal border perennial. Its spikes of small, iris-like, red flowers are a familiar late summer sight in many a modern garden but it should be remembered that in its southern African homeland, it is a plant of stream banks and* similar moist places, and I feel that it is in such spots that it is seen to best advantage. But there's no denying its vigour (especially of the true species; the named varieties are rather more domesticated), and it should definitely not be placed in small water gardens where it will very quickly become out of hand and difficult to deal with. **"**

SITE Full sun to light shade.
PREFERRED SOIL Most, but preferably fairly light, light to almost moderate moisture.
HARDINESS Very hardy, tolerating -20°C (-4°F).
SIZE Will attain 50-60 x 20-25cm (20-24 x 8-10in) after three or four years.

RECOMMENDED VARIETIES
The normal species is much the most widely available but it is wise to seek out the named varieties: *alba*, white; 'Jennifer', large flowers, pink; 'Major', rich red; 'Mrs Hegarty', pale pink, old but good; 'Professor Barnard', dark red; 'Viscountess Byng', pink.

CARE
Mulch in spring and in autumn and give a balanced general fertilizer in spring. Divide every two or three years.
PROPAGATION
By division in spring.
PROBLEMS
None.

Schizostylis coccinea 'Vicountess Byng'

BOG PLANTS

Stylophorum diphyllum Wood poppy

❝ *I am baffled as to why this lovely North American yellow-flowered poppy is seen so rarely cultivated in gardens, for it does seem to combine the best features of two related and much more familiar genera. It has the foliage and perennial habit of the greater celandine,* Chelidonium, *but possesses the much more attractive flowers of the annual Welsh Poppy. You are unlikely to see it, if at all, being suggested as a bog garden plant but its requirement of wet soils and shaded sites make it an admirable addition. If you are fortunate, its flowering period will coincide with that of* Geranium phaeum. **❞**

CARE
Mulch in autumn and spring and give a balanced general fertilizer in spring. Cut down top growth in autumn.

SITE Light to moderate shade.
PREFERRED SOIL Moderately rich, light moisture.
HARDINESS Moderately hardy to hardy, tolerating around -15°C (5°F).
SIZE Will attain 30-45 x 30-45cm (12-18 x 12-18in) after three or four years.

RECOMMENDED VARIETIES
Normal species only is available although a related and rather similar Chinese species, *Stylophorum lasiocarpum*, is seen sometimes.

PROPAGATION
By division in spring, or by seed sown in soil-based compost with slight bottom heat.

PROBLEMS
None.

Symplocarpus foetidus Polecat weed

❝ *This is one of the oddest of plants. The leaves are typical of the arum family, but it is the flowers that are so odd. The spathe is hood-like, yellowish-green, with red spots in that sickly aroid fashion, and foetid too. It generates its own warmth and so protects itself from frost damage despite flowering early in the year and in cold places.* **❞**

Symplocarpus foetidus

Stylophorum diphyllum

SITE Full sun to moderate shade.
PREFERRED SOIL Moderately rich, organic, moderate to almost high moisture.
HARDINESS Very hardy, tolerating -20°C (-4°F).
SIZE Will attain about 25 x 25cm (10 x 10in) after about three years.

CARE
Mulch in autumn and then lightly in spring just as the leaves emerge. Give a balanced general fertilizer in spring. Top growth may either be cut back in autumn or left to die down naturally.

PROPAGATION
By division in late autumn but this must be done carefully as the plant resents disturbance.

PROBLEMS
None.

RECOMMENDED VARIETIES
Normal species only is available.

Thalictrum flavum

Thalictrum flavum
Yellow meadow rue

❝ *Several thalictrums or meadow rues make suitable bog garden plants but I think this is one of the most successful. It is a tall and graceful plant for placing towards the back of a mixed planting, with bluish-green leaves and masses of yellow flowers that give the appearance of fluffy feathery heads.* ❞

CARE
Mulch in the autumn and the spring and give a balanced general fertilizer in the spring. Cut down the top growth in the autumn. The stems may well require staking unless they are planted around with a ring of stiffer stemmed plants of equal or similar height which can provide constant support as the plant grows.

PROPAGATION
By division of the fully grown plants in late autumn or, even better, in the spring.

PROBLEMS
None.

SITE Full sun to light shade.
PREFERRED SOIL Tolerates most, but best in deep and moderately rich soils, light moisture.
HARDINESS Very hardy, tolerating -20°C (-4°F).
SIZE 1.2-1.5m x 45-50cm (4-5ft x 18-20in) after three years.

RECOMMENDED VARIETIES
A form, *glaucum*, is available with rather bluer foliage and a variety called 'Illuminator' may be seen. This has bright green leaves but much paler yellow flowers.

BOG PLANTS

Tiarella cordifolia Foam flower

❝ *Tiarellas are relatively uncommon in gardens yet really quite versatile. I have them in some of the drier, as well as the wetter parts of my own garden. Like a number of the other species in this book, they demonstrate the wide range of plants that exists in the saxifrage family. The flowers are individually tiny but collectively very pretty, almost, I suppose, foam-like. They appear in early summer above very fresh, rounded, crinkly leaves. This is a good plant and undeserving of neglect.* ❞

CARE
Mulch in autumn and spring and give a balanced general fertilizer in spring. In very conspicuous places, the dead flower stems may be cut back but, otherwise, are better left.

PROPAGATION
By division in spring or autumn.

SITE Moderate to deep shade.
PREFERRED SOIL Tolerates most, light moisture.
HARDINESS Very hardy, tolerating -20°C (-4°F).
SIZE Will attain 15-25 x 25-45cm (6-10 x 10-18in), depending on species, after three or four years.

RECOMMENDED VARIETIES
Tiarella cordifolia is the most frequently seen species but it can become rather invasive in moist rich soil. *T. wherryi* (still sometimes called *T. collina*) doesn't have spreading stolons and is much more compact. *T. polyphylla* is a slightly more robust oriental plant (the others are North American) and is similarly much less invasive.

PROBLEMS
None.

Tiarella cordifolia

Tradescantia virginiana Spiderwort

❝ *Most gardeners still think of tradescantias as houseplants, and they are much more likely to be seen in the bathroom than the bog garden. But to restrict your thinking in this way is to deny yourself the pleasure of growing some very attractive flowering and foliage perennials. The leaves are narrow and almost grass-like, the flowers characteristic and three-petalled in a rather wide range of colours. The main problem that I have with tradescantias is that their habit is rather untidy and sprawing, as might well befit a wilder garden, but the way that their flowers are borne is somewhat formal.* ❞

SITE Full sun to a very light shade.
PREFERRED SOIL Tolerates most but best in fairly rich, organic soils, light moisture.
HARDINESS Hardy, tolerating around -15°C (5°F).
SIZE Will attain about 30-40 x 30-40cm (12-16 x 12-16in) after three years.

CARE
Mulch lightly in autumn and spring and give a balanced general fertilizer in spring. Must be tidied up after flowering if they are grown in conspicuous places and are best divided every two or three years.

PROPAGATION

By softwood cuttings taken in spring for rooting in humus-enriched, soil-based compost or alternatively by division in spring.

PROBLEMS

Mildew.

RECOMMENDED VARIETIES

There are many hybrids, probably derived from this species and generally listed under it or as T. x andersoniana. Among the most striking are 'Innocence', white; 'Isis', dark blue; 'Osprey', white with bluish-purple centre; 'Purple Dome', deep purple and 'Zwanenburg Blue', large, clear mid-blue.

Tradescantia virginiana

Tricyrtis hirta
Toad lily

" Some years ago, I remember visiting a very famous garden with a very famous gardener. There was a clump of toad lilies growing in a damp corner of a small woodland, and my famous friend didn't know what it was. But this was less a reflection on him than on the plant, for it is only very recently that it has become at all well known. Once seen, however, it is not forgotten, having perhaps more of an exotic, orchid-like appearance than almost any bulb likely to be growing in a temperate climate. It's hard to believe that anything with flowers of such a dramatic spidery shape and in shades of sinister purple can be hardy. "

SITE Light to deep shade.
PREFERRED SOIL Tolerates most but best in rich, organic soils, light moisture.
HARDINESS Hardy, tolerating around -15°C (5°F).
SIZE Will attain 75-90 x 45-60cm (30-34 x 18-24in) after four years.

CARE

Mulch in autumn and spring and give a balanced general fertilizer in spring. Cut off dead heads after flowering and leave undisturbed once established.

PROPAGATION

By division in spring (if you don't mind disturbing the clumps) or from seed sown fresh in soil-based compost in a

Tricyrtis latifolia

RECOMMENDED VARIETIES

The normal species has white flowers with masses of purple spots and among the common variants are *Tricyrtis hirta alba*, with more or less white flowers, 'Miyazaki', which is rather more vigorous with arching stems and 'Variegata', with golden edges to the leaves. Related species that are almost as hardy include T. formosana with white or pale yellow flowers with red spots and, my favourite, T. latifolia with yellowish-green flowers with purple spots.

cold-frame. Some seed companies now sell packeted seed of mixed hybrids but it is not easy to germinate, even after stratifying.

PROBLEMS

None.

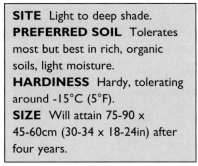

BOG PLANTS

Trollius Globe flower

❝*I have always confused* Trollius *with* Caltha *but I don't think this so outrageous a confusion because they are both, in effect, large bog garden, spring-flowering buttercups. Both have golden flowers, and the easiest way to tell them apart (I simply must remember this) is that while* Caltha *has shiny, glossy leaves, those of* Trollius *are divided and much more buttercup-like.* Trollius *are also considerably taller and, rather to my regret, have been hybridized and selected for forms that vary quite considerably in colour from the lovely wild plant.*❞

SIMILAR SPECIES
Trollius chinensis, a tall, asiatic, summer-flowering species with a central tuft of orange stamens, best known as the selected form 'Golden Queen'. *T. pumilus*, a superb, lower-growing Himalayan species with yellowish-orange flowers with dark red exteriors.

CARE
Mulch in autumn and spring and give a balanced general fertilizer in spring. Cut back dead flower heads if practicable as this tends to encourage a second flush of flowers in the late summer or early autumn.

PROPAGATION
By division in spring or autumn.

PROBLEMS
Mildew, but not usually until after flowering is completed.

SITE
Full sun to light shade.
PREFERRED SOIL
Tolerates most, ideally with a light to moderate moisture.
HARDINESS
Very hardy, tolerating -20°C (-4°F).
SIZE
Varies with species: *T. europaeus* and the hybrids will mostly attain about 75 x 45cm (30 x 18in) after three or four years; *T. chinensis*, slightly more and *T. pumilus*, about half of this.

Trollius europaeus

RECOMMENDED VARIETIES
My preference remains for the native European *Trollius europaeus* with its lovely globe-like, golden-yellow flowers. If rather more fiery hues appeal to you, you will like some of the somewhat inaccurately named hybrids derived from it, usually grouped under the name *T. x cultorum*: 'Earliest of All', golden-yellow, early; 'Feuertroll' ('Fireglobe'), deep orange; 'Golden Queen', orange; 'Goldquelle', yellow; 'Orange Princess', orange-yellow.

Uvularia Merry bells

❝*There's a cheerful name for a cheerful plant, but one that seems to cheer far fewer gardeners than it should, for this isn't a well-known species. It is a close, North American relative of a plant that is much more widely grown, the Solomon's seal, and yet its dangling flowers are much prettier. It also suffers little, if at all, from that curse of the real Solomon's seals, the leaf-stripping sawfly. I would like to see it grown more extensively.*❞

SITE
Moderate to deep shade.
PREFERRED SOIL
Preferably organic, rich, light moisture.
HARDINESS
Very hardy, tolerating -20°C (-4°F).
SIZE
Will attain about 60 x 25cm (24 x 10in) after three or four years.

CARE
Mulch in autumn and spring and give a balanced general fertilizer in spring. Cut down old flower stems in autumn.

PROPAGATION
By division in the spring or by sowing fresh seed in a humus-enriched, soil-based compost in the autumn in a cold-frame.

PROBLEMS
None.

RECOMMENDED VARIETIES
The only species likely to be available is the best, *Uvularia grandiflora*.

Uvularia grandiflora

Veratrum nigrum

Veratrum

" *While no truly black plant exists, I have a list of species with very dark flowers or foliage. On the floral list I include this one, although it is easily seen to be a very dark purple. It is a rhizome-forming member of the lily family and is a tall, rather stately and imposing species for the shaded bog garden where its branched spikes of flowers will persist for much of the summer.* "

SITE Light to moderate shade.
PREFERRED SOIL Preferably organic, fairly rich, light moisture.
HARDINESS Very hardy, tolerating -20°C (-4°F).
SIZE In good conditions, will attain up to 2m x 75cm (6ft x 30in) after three or four years.

CARE
Mulch in autumn and spring and give a balanced general fertilizer in spring. Cut down old flower stems when flowers fade. Should be grown in a sheltered position where staking is not necessary.

PROPAGATION
By division in the spring or, better, because mature plants resent disturbance, by sowing fresh seed in a humus-enriched, soil-based compost in autumn in a cold-frame.

PROBLEMS
None.

RECOMMENDED VARIETIES
The species *Veratrum nigrum* is the only one likely to be seen.

FERNS

By and large, ferns are plants of damp places, although dampness of atmosphere is generally more important for them than dampness of soil and it comes as a surprise when ferns die as a result of their roots and rhizomes rotting in very wet soil. They also tend to be plants of shady places and not many thrive in full exposure to hot sun. For these reasons, while there are a number of bog garden species, there are perhaps not as many as might be expected. I have described ferns in some detail and recommended a considerable number of species in Book 3 of the series (*Best Shade Plants*), and many of these will be successful in the slightly drier areas towards the edge of the bog garden. In this book I shall concentrate on those that really are the most appropriate for water garden conditions and only briefly outline their biology.

Ferns are unlike almost any other plants that you are likely to grow in your garden in that they lack flowers and seeds and reproduce instead by means of spores (which are often visible *en masse* as small, variously shaped, brownish pustules on the undersides of the fronds). They make up for their lack of floral appeal, however, by having a wide variety of frond shapes and sizes, although most are more or less indented in outline (and, of course, this shape has given rise to the term 'ferny' being used to describe the leaves of other types of plant that have this general appearance). There are probably almost equal numbers of deciduous and evergreen species for garden use. Raising your own ferns from spores can be done and is most rewarding and I have described the technique in *Best Shade Plants* but can't pretend that it is as easy as raising plants from seed. Most of the best named varieties of fern, moreover, must be propagated vegetatively and almost certainly, therefore, you will obtain your new stock as bought plants.

Dryopteris dilatata Broad buckler fern

" *I'm surprised that fern nurseries and water gardeners don't grow this fern more commonly, for it is an almost ever-present inhabitant of marshes, fens and other naturally wet habitats. Even in its wild form it is at least as attractive as some other cultivated species with its rather closely tufted habit and narrowly-elongated, fresh green, deciduous fronds. Some of these cultivated variants are very striking and distinctly beautiful. An added bonus is that this fern has the merit of being perhaps the most highly shade-tolerant of all the water garden ferns, as anyone who has found it nestling in among natural reed swamps will almost certainly testify.* "

CARE
Mulch in autumn and spring and give a light dressing of balanced general fertilizer or bonemeal in spring. Leave dead fronds in place over winter and then cut them back in spring just before the new growth begins to expand.

SITE Moderate to deep shade.
PREFERRED SOIL Organic, preferably acidic, moderate to high moisture.
HARDINESS Very hardy, tolerating -20°C (-4°F).
SIZE Normal species will attain 1.2-1.5m x 60-90cm (4-5ft x 24-34in) after three or four years; the named forms reach approximately one-third of this.

PROPAGATION
By division in spring.
PROBLEMS
None.

RECOMMENDED VARIETIES
The normal species, *Dryopteris dilatata,* is most commonly available but among the best forms are 'Crispa Whiteside' with attractive wavy fronds and curled edges and 'Lepidota Cristata' with very finely divided fronds with minute lacy crests. A related species *D. carthusiana,* the narrow buckler fern, is also sometimes seen. One other good *Dryopteris* for moderate soil moisture is *D. wallichiana* with a beautiful, almost black stem.

Matteuccia struthiopteris
Shuttlecock fern

" This is a highly distinctive and appropriately named decidu- ous fern with rather closely placed, markedly upright fronds that do, indeed, look like tall green shuttlecocks. The alterna- tive common name is ostrich fern, for the individual fronds do bear a passing resemblance to ostrich feathers. It occurs sparsely in the wild in Europe, but it isn't a British native although, with its somewhat aggressive behaviour, I'm surprised that it hasn't become naturalized long before now, for it is distinctly invasive with long, very adventurous rhi- zomes. It should only be planted, therefore, where it can be prop- erly accommodated. "

SITE Light to moderate shade.
PREFERRED SOIL Tolerates most, preferably but not essen- tially humus-rich, moderate to high moisture.
HARDINESS Very hardy, tolerating -20°C (-4°F).
SIZE Will attain up to 1m x 75-90cm (3ft x 30-34in) after two or three years but spreads much more widely in time.

RECOMMENDED VARIETIES
Normal species only is available; there are no named varieties, although there are one or two related species which may occasionally be offered.

PROBLEMS
None.

CARE
Mulch in autumn and spring and give a balanced general fertilizer or bone- meal in spring. Cut back dead fronds in spring before new growth expands. Dig out stray plants.

PROPAGATION
By division in spring; simply sever the rhizomes connecting the parent to the daughter plant; these may well arise a metre or more away from the original parent plant.

Dryopteris dilatata

Matteuccia struthiopteris

FERNS

Onoclea sensiblis Sensitive fern

❝ *I love this fern but I just wish it would last a little longer each autumn. Its common name gives the clue, for although its rootstock is perfectly tough and hardy, its fronds are very frost-sensitive and will turn brown and shrivel as soon as the temperature drops below freezing. It is also rather slow to unfold in spring and even then can be set back by a late frost. Obtaining the full benefit of it each year is, therefore, something of a lottery although it is nonetheless a good plant for stabilizing stream banks. The fronds are pretty and are roughly triangular in form, with a pinkish tinge when first they emerge in spring.* ❞

SITE Light to moderate shade.
PREFERRED SOIL Ideally organic and slightly acidic, moderate to high moisture.
HARDINESS Very hardy, tolerating -20°C (-4°F).
SIZE Will attain about 60 x 90cm (24 x 34in) after three or four years.

RECOMMENDED VARIETIES
The normal species is usually the only form available, although a selected, rather coppery-coloured variant may occasionally be found as well.

CARE
Mulch in the autumn and spring and give a light dressing of balanced general fertilizer or bonemeal in spring.

Cut back the dead fronds either in the autumn or early spring. Leave undisturbed once properly established in place.
PROPAGATION
By division in spring.
PROBLEMS
None.

Osmunda regalis Royal fern

❝ *With the exception of the so-called tree ferns,* Osmunda *is without doubt the most spectacularly hardy fern that most temperate climate gardeners are ever likely to see. It is also unquestionably the finest European native species, although relatively few people will see it growing wild for it is found only on wet fen or marsh banks. At one time, orchid growers were most familiar with it, in name at least, for the roots were used as the source of the osmunda fibre in which orchids were potted. Fortunately, bark-based composts have now taken their place and the deciduous osmundas have been left in peace. The feathery, sterile fronds fan outwards as if embracing the tall, stiff, spore-bearing, fertile fronds that arise from the very centre of the crown.* ❞

CARE
Mulch in autumn and spring and give a light dressing of balanced general fertilizer or bonemeal in spring. Leave dead fronds in place over winter and then cut them back in spring before new growth begins to expand.
PROPAGATION
By division in spring, although dividing a full grown osmunda is no task for the faint-hearted and simply chopping off a portion of the crown may be all that is possible.
PROBLEMS
None.

Onoclea sensiblis

Osmunda regalis

SITE Full sun to light or moderate shade.
PREFERRED SOIL Organic, acidic, moderate to high moisture.
HARDINESS Very hardy, tolerating -20°C (-4°F).
SIZE Will attain 2 x 2m (6 x 6ft) after three or four years.

RECOMMENDED VARIETIES
The normal species only is usually available, although there are a few selected variants including crested and wavy-leaved forms. The commonest variety, however, is a lovely, lower-growing plant called *purpurascens* which has purple stems and markedly brown-pink young growths. One or two related but smaller and less spectacular North American or Asian species may also sometimes be seen.

Thelypteris palustris Marsh fern

❝ *A plant called the marsh fern must be a strong candidate for the bog garden although, in truth, it is only its requirement for very wet conditions that justifies its inclusion. It is a good basic fern, not very different in appearance from a good many other species. The fronds arise individually rather than in tufts and, for this reason, the clumps can seem rather untidy; however, it does revel in the wet and, being a British and European native, it makes a good choice for water gardens where local species are preferred and where its rather invasive habit can be tolerated.* ❞

CARE
Mulch in autumn and spring and give a light dressing of balanced general

SITE Full sun to light or moderate shade.
PREFERRED SOIL Organic, preferably slightly acidic, moderate to high moisture.
HARDINESS Very hardy, tolerating -20°C (-4°F).
SIZE Will attain 1m x 75m (3ft x 30in) after three years.

RECOMMENDED VARIETIES
Normal species only is available.

fertilizer or bonemeal in spring. Leave dead fronds in place over winter and then cut them back in spring just before new growth brings about expansion once again.

PROPAGATION
By division in spring.

PROBLEMS
None.

Thelypteris palustris

GRASSES

I have deliberately stretched my definitions here to include plants from three superficially similar but quite distinct families: the true grasses, the sedges, and the rushes. All play rather comparable roles in the water garden and embrace marginal and bog garden types, with one or two almost true aquatics. All three include some most attractive variegated forms and, with several species, it is these alone that I describe and recommend. Indeed, with almost all of these plants, it tends to be the foliage that sells them although some do have very pretty flowering heads too.

A good rule of thumb to help you distinguish between the three groups is to look at the leaves in cross-section. Those of the true grasses are flat or 'V'-shaped, those of the sedges triangular and those of the rushes generally circular. It doesn't apply in every case but it will help until you gain experience.

Alopecurus pratensis 'Aureovariegatus'
Meadow foxtail grass

* Don't be misled by the common name, 'meadow grass', as the term meadow can be taken to embrace water meadows too, for this is a versatile and adaptable species that is common in its plain-leaved form throughout much of the temperate northern hemisphere. It is slightly but not annoyingly invasive and in early summer, produces the most delightful, soft, cylindrical inflorescence with a gentle purple flush. The leaves are superb with the most vividly gold stripes of any grass that I know.*

SITE Bog garden, full sun to light shade.
PREFERRED SOIL Tolerates most, low moisture.
HARDINESS Very hardy, tolerating -20°C (-4°F).
SIZE Attains 45 x 30cm (18 x 12in) after three or four years.

RECOMMENDED VARIETIES
The variegated form only of this plant is recommended, although there is a less vigorous but rather remarkable sport derived from it called 'Aureus' in which the leaves are an astonishing pure gold colour.

CARE
Mulch in autumn and spring and give a balanced general fertilizer in spring. Leave top growth in autumn until the winter weather lays it low and then cut it right back to the crown. Divide approximately every three or four years.

PROPAGATION
By division in spring or autumn.

PROBLEMS
None.

Alopecurus pratensis 'Aureovariegatus'

Carex elata 'Aurea' **Tufted Sedge**

❝ Anyone who knows the sedges will realize that calling a plant 'the tufted sedge' is a pretty imprecise description, as a large number of species develop in a tufted shape. Nonetheless, take the name at face value for it does mean that the species forms into discrete clumps and therefore isn't invasive. The separate male and female inflorescences are somewhat uninspiring but the leaves have the most attractive yellow margins, although the colour does tend to fade to green as the summer progresses. ❞

CARE

Mulch in autumn and spring and give a balanced general fertilizer in spring. Leave the top growth over winter. Divide occasionally; every five or six years should be sufficient.

PROPAGATION

By division in spring or autumn.

RECOMMENDED VARIETIES

The variegated form only is recommended and it is sometimes to be found under the name 'Bowles' Golden'.

PROBLEMS

None.

SITE Bog garden, full sun to light shade.
PREFERRED SOIL Tolerates most, low moisture.
HARDINESS Very hardy, tolerating -20°C (4°F).
SIZE Will attain 45-50 x 45-50cm (18-20 x 18-20in) after four or five years.

OTHER VERY HARDY *CAREX* SPECIES FOR THE BOG GARDEN (EXCLUDING VERY VIGOROUS OR INVASIVE TYPES):

Carex morrowii 'Variegata' is perhaps the best of a few variegated forms of a fairly robust, tufted, Japanese species (up to 35 x 25cm (14 x 10in)) with rough, stiff dark green leaves with white margins. It seems to flower only occasionally. *C. pseudocyperus* is one of the commonest of sedges throughout the temperate regions of the world and one that may be grown as a marginal as well as in the wetter parts of the bog garden. It has a loosely tufted habit, pale green leaves and very pretty, pendulous, green female inflorescences. Attains up to 75 x 30cm (30 x 12in). The tufted European species *C. sylvatica*, despite its name of wood sedge, is a good plant for the drier parts of the bog garden and is also extremely shade tolerant. The inflorescences are very dainty, the females being especially pendulous and fluttering attractively in the breeze. It normally attains a maximum size of around 50 x 25cm (20 x 10in).

Carex elata 'Aurea'

GRASSES

Cortaderia selloana Pampas grass

❝ *Whatever is to be done about pampas grass? Clearly, it causes gardeners all manner of problems: it won't flower, it grows too big, and should it be burned in the winter or just have the dead growth pulled out? And, in any event, surely the South American pampas grasslands are dry, so what is the plant doing in a book about water gardening? Well, yes, the grasslands are dry for much of the year but they can also be jolly wet at times and the cortaderias, in practice, are versatile plants, tolerating a wide range of soil types. They also have the great virtue of being among the few large grasses that will grow in a bog garden and yet are clump-forming and not invasive. So, if you choose your variety carefully it will be bound to have my endorsement.* ❞

SITE Bog garden, full sun to light shade.
PREFERRED SOIL Tolerates most, low moisture.
HARDINESS Very hardy, tolerating -20°C (-4°F).
SIZE Varies (see Recommended Varieties) up 3 x 2m (10 x 6ft).

RECOMMENDED VARIETIES
The choice of variety is most important if you want a plant of known size that will produce flowers. Un-named seedling plants very often do not flower so always choose a named variety from a reputable source.

'Aureolineata' (sometimes called 'Gold Band'), a really lovely plant, leaves with yellowish-gold edges, up to 2m (6ft); 'Pumila', only up to 1.5m (5ft), good flower production; 'Sunningdale Silver', silver-white flower heads, to 2.5-3m (8-10ft).

CARE
Mulch in the autumn and the spring and give a balanced general fertilizer in the spring. Leave top growth on in autumn as the dead flower heads are most attractive during the winter. Cut down in early spring but *don't* set fire to the clump as you are more than likely to kill it. It is far better to don a pair of very stout gloves and pull out the dead material. Leave undisturbed once fully established.

PROPAGATION
By division in spring.

PROBLEMS
None.

Cortaderia selloana

Cyperus sedges

❝ Cyperus *is one of the largest genera in the sedge family, although temperate climate gardeners and botanists will have a distorted impression of its importance, for the bulk of the species are from warm areas of the world. Relatively few, in consequence, are common or good garden plants but I include here three that I rate highly for the water garden. Their most distinctive feature is that the inflorescence is their crowning glory; quite literally, for it takes a crown or umbrella-like form.* ❞

SITE Marginal or bog garden (see Recommended Varieties), full sun to light shade.
PREFERRED SOIL Tolerates most, moderate to high moisture.
HARDINESS Fairly hardy, tolerating -10 to -15°C (14 to 5°F), except *C. involucratus*, barely hardy, tolerating only about -5°C (23°F).
SIZE Varies (see Recommended varieties) up to 3 x 2m (10-6ft).

CARE
C. eragrostis and *C. longus*: mulch in the autumn and the spring and give a balanced general fertilizer in the spring. Leave top growth on in the autumn but cut down as soon as the winter weather takes its toll; those umbrella-like heads are prone to take a battering from the wind and rain. Divide every four or five years or, in wilder gardens, leave undisturbed.

C. involucratus: not hardy enough to leave outdoors all year round except in very mild areas, so grow in large pots and take in for greenhouse protection in winter.

PROPAGATION

By division in spring.

PROBLEMS

None.

RECOMMENDED VARIETIES

Cyperus involucratus (also called *C. alternifolius* and commonly known as umbrella plant, or Nile grass), slender floral rays with the leaf-like bracts forming a 'nest' from which the rays emerge. Up to 1m x 30cm (3ft x 12in) after three years. A marginal plant.

C. eragrostis, inflorescence compound, subdivided and graceful, up to 90 x 30cm (34 x 12in) after three years. Bog garden, moderate moisture.

C. longus, a loose, open flower head above lush green leaves, up to 1.5m x 50cm (5ft x 20in). A marginal plant.

Eleocharis acicularis
Needle spike rush

❝ *A widespread and common, small and very slender little rush with, appropriately, needle-like leaves that produces small, discrete tufts but is deceptively invasive and spreads rather widely when you aren't looking. It's a versatile plant that will grow* either as a bog garden species, when it bears tiny inflorescences, or as a marginal in shallow water when, like some other marginals, it obstinately refuses to flower. In the wild, it grows at the edge of pools that dry up in summer and then bursts into bloom. ❞

SITE Marginal or bog garden, full sun to light shade.

PREFERRED SOIL Tolerates most, but preferably acidic, low to high moisture.

HARDINESS Very hardy, tolerating -20°C (-4°F).

SIZE Varies, depending on its growing position; up to 50cm (20in) when grown as a marginal but rarely more than 10cm (4in) when out of standing water.

CARE

If grown in the bog garden, mulch in the autumn and thr spring and give a balanced general fertilizer in the spring. Do not cut it back in the autumn. Divide approximately every three or four years if it is necessary to limit the plant's spread.

PROPAGATION

By division in spring.

PROBLEMS

None.

RECOMMENDED VARIETIES

Normal species only is available although a related and similar plant, *Eleocharis palustris*, that tends to be rather more invasive, may also be seen sometimes.

Cyperus involucratus

Cyperus longus

GRASSES

Eriophorum angustifolium
Cotton grass

❝ *This is the plant that, more than any other, conjures up for me images of the high-altitude pools, streams and marshes of the British mountains, for, in summer (the only time that most people are likely to go to such places), large swathes of ground are bedecked with its nodding, cottony, white flower heads. Despite its name, it is, in reality, not a true grass but a species of sedge and it isn't the easiest of plants to cultivate in low-altitude water gardens. It really both looks and grows best in large, semi-wild gardens in conditions that approximate to its natural home.* ❞

SITE Bog garden, full sun to light shade.
PREFERRED SOIL Acidic, preferably organic, moderate to high moisture.
HARDINESS Very hardy, tolerating -20°C (-4°F).
SIZE Will attain a height of about 75 x 25cm (30 x 12in) after three years.

RECOMMENDED VARIETIES
Normal species only is generally available although one or two related species may sometimes be seen.

CARE
Mulch in autumn and spring if possible until well established and longer if the area has any tendency to dry out in summer. Give a very light dressing of a balanced general fertilizer in the spring, at least until it is established.

Allow flower stems to die down naturally. Leave undisturbed once the plant is fully established.

PROPAGATION
By division in spring or by seed sown in a wet, humus-enriched, soil-based compost in spring.

PROBLEMS
None.

Eriophorum angustifolium

Glyceria maxima
'Variegata'
Reed sweet grass

❝ *This is one of the most adaptable and easy to grow of grasses. It was, I think, the first ornamental grass that I ever grew and I soon learned the lesson of not planting it in a moist herbaceous border unless you are prepared to divide and restrain it regularly. Its natural home, however, is at the side of streams and other water-courses, and it is equally aggressive there. But, at the end of the day, those green and white striped leaves are extremely pretty, so my advice must be to resist it if you have limited space, but entrust it to colonize (and indeed stabilize) larger, wilder areas if you have the room.* ❞

SITE Bog garden, or shallow-water marginal, full sun to light shade.
PREFERRED SOIL Tolerates most, low to high moisture.
HARDINESS Very hardy, tolerating -20°C (-4°F).
SIZE Will attain approximately 75 x 50cm (30 x 20in) after one or two years.

CARE
Mulch in the autumn and the spring until established. Give a light dressing of a balanced general fertilizer in spring, at least until established. Assuming it is in a fairly wild area, the

Glyceria maxima **'Variegata'**

top growth may be allowed to die down naturally. Divide as often as necessary to contain its enthusiasm.

PROPAGATION
By division in spring or autumn.

PROBLEMS
None.

RECOMMENDED VARIETIES
The variegated form is the only one recommended.

Hakonechloa macra

❝ *I'd like to bet that, despite its name,* Hakonechloa *is one of the best-selling ornamental grasses. It will, as nursery-owners tend to put it, 'sell on sight'. It is Japanese, soft-foliaged and, in its best forms, beautifully variegated and tolerant of light shade. It isn't quite what I would call an informal grass, however, and its appearance really looks most appropriate in the more formal bog garden. As it isn't a very invasive species, it makes a good plant for smaller gardens too, which must be one of the reasons why it has become so popular.* **❞**

CARE
Mulch in autumn and spring and give a dressing of a balanced general fertilizer in spring. Divide every three or four years.

PROPAGATION
By division in spring or autumn.

PROBLEM
None.

Hakonechloa macra **'Aureola'**

SITE Bog garden, full sun to light shade.
PREFERRED SOIL Tolerates most, low moisture.
HARDINESS Very hardy, tolerating -20°C (-4°F).
SIZE Will attain approximately 25 x 40cm (10-16in) after three or four years.

RECOMMENDED VARIETIES
The two variegated forms are 'Alboaurea', with a yellow and white leaf striping; and the better known 'Aureola' with beautiful, striking golden-yellow and bright green stripes.

Hakonechloa macra

GRASSES

Holcus mollis 'Albovariegatus' Creeping soft grass

❝ *Yes, it is soft, and yes, it creeps but the variegated form creeps much less than the true species. It has a rather unusual leaf appearance, for while there are several grasses with white-striped leaves, this one simply has white edges. It is a lovely thing although, in common with many variegated species, it flowers less reliably than its parent form. It makes an ideal edging for a lightly shaded corner.* ❞

SITE Bog garden, full sun to light shade.
PREFERRED SOIL Tolerates most, low moisture.
HARDINESS Very hardy, tolerating -20°C (-4°F).
SIZE Will attain a height of about 30 x 50cm (12 x 20in) after three or four years.

RECOMMENDED VARIETIES
The variegated species only is recommended; the normal green form is an invasive weed and is best avoided.

CARE
Mulch lightly in autumn and spring and give a light dressing of a balanced general fertilizer in spring. Trim with shears after flowering. Divide every three or four years.

PROPAGATION
By division in spring or autumn.

PROBLEMS
None.

Holcus mollis 'Albovariegatus'

Juncus effusus 'Spiralis' Corkscrew rush

❝ *There are a good many 'spiral' or 'corkscrew' trees and shrubs in the garden, but a rush with twisted and contorted stems is much rarer. It creates an appearance that is interesting rather than lovely. The normal species, a widely distributed plant, the so-called soft rush, is a thing of no garden merit but a place should certainly be found for this curiosity, if only to prove that the bog garden can supply botanical fascination to match the best.* ❞

SITE Bog garden, full sun to light shade.
PREFERRED SOIL Tolerates most, low moisture.
HARDINESS Very hardy, tolerating -20°C (-4°F).
SIZE Will attain a height of about 30 x 50cm (12 x 20in) after three or four years.

CARE
Mulch lightly in autumn and spring and give a dressing of a balanced general fertilizer in spring. Divide every three or four years.

PROPAGATION
By division in spring or autumn.

PROBLEMS
None.

RECOMMENDED VARIETIES
The spiral form is the only one recommended.

Juncus effusus 'Spiralis'

SITE Bog garden, full sun to light or moderate shade.
PREFERRED SOIL Tolerates most, low moisture.
HARDINESS Very hardy, tolerating -20°C (-4°F).
SIZE Will attain 30-45 x 30-45cm (12-18 x 12-18in) after three or four years.

RECOMMENDED VARIETIES

Luzula nivea (snowy woodrush), which has rather broad leaves for a rush, with lovely, dense, white inflorescences. *L. sylvatica* (also known as *L. maxima*) with fresh, lush foliage in a range of colour variants, most notably 'Aurea', which is yellowish-gold; and 'Marginata', a deep rich green with white edges.

PROPAGATION

By division in spring or autumn.

PROBLEMS

None.

Luzula Woodrush

CARE

Mulch lightly in the autumn and the spring and give a light dressing of a balanced general fertilizer in spring. Divide every three or four years.

" Luzula is one of those genera better known for its weed species than for its ornamentals. Given that the commonest weed Luzula is the field woodrush (there's a plant that can't make up its mind where it belongs), a plant of dry, impoverished, acidic lawns, it comes as something of a surprise to learn that it has relatives thriving in the wet. Yet two species especially are widely tolerant of different soil types and make good garden plants; and one, indeed, has given rise to a number of selected varieties. Both are of tufted habit and taller than the lawn weed, and both have some extremely pretty white or greenish flower heads. "

Luzula nivea

GRASSES

Milium effusum 'Aureum' Wood Millet

66 One of my very favourite grasses, even though it tends to be relatively short-lived. It will generally self-seed, however, and so a planting in a semi-wild garden should perpetuate itself. The normal species is a fairly common, European woodland grass of no real merit but the golden-foliaged variant is a really choice plant. In a slightly shaded bog garden, it looks wonderful with the dappled, early morning sun filtering through the tree canopy and catching its lovely leaves and delicate, trembling flower heads. 99

SITE Bog garden, light to almost moderate shade.
PREFERRED SOIL Tolerates most, low moisture.
HARDINESS Very hardy, tolerating -20°C (-4°F).
SIZE Will attain approximately 30 x 50cm (12 x 20in) after three or four years.

RECOMMENDED VARIETIES
The golden-foliaged variety is the only one recommended.

CARE
Mulch lightly in autumn and spring, at least until well established and give a light dressing of a balanced general fertilizer in spring. Leave to die down naturally after flowering. Leave undisturbed once established.

PROPAGATION
By division in spring or autumn.

PROBLEMS
None.

Milium effusum 'Aureum'

Miscanthus sinensis

66 The species of Miscanthus are among the giants of the grass family. Indeed, apart from the bamboos, I can't think of any taller, hardy grasses, for some of them reach 4m (13ft) in height. The species described here is tall, although not that tall, but it does include some of the finest of all coloured-foliage forms of any large grass. It is very much at home in the bog garden although, a bad competitor there, for its clump-forming habit places it at a disadvantage against more vigorous, shorter-growing but more widely-spreading species. Choose its companions carefully. 99

SITE Bog garden, full sun to light shade.
PREFERRED SOIL Tolerates most, low to almost high moisture content.
HARDINESS Very hardy, tolerating -20°C (-4°F).
SIZE Varies with variety from 1.5-3m x 75-90cm (5-10ft x 30-34in) after three or four years.

CARE
Mulch in autumn and spring, and give a dressing of a balanced general fertilizer in spring. Leave to die down naturally after flowering. Leave undisturbed once established.

PROPAGATION
By division in spring or autumn.

PROBLEMS
None.

Miscanthus sinensis '**Variegatus**'

Molinia caerulea Moor grass

" *Two accurate names, moor grass because it is indeed a very common plant of open, damp, acid moorland, and* caerulea *because, from a distance, there is a distinct bluish flush to the plants although they appear green or brown when* examined individually at close quarters. There's no doubt, however, that it is at its most attractive when planted in large numbers in an open space, and it is a species that looks a little lost and forlorn when on its own. "

CARE

Mulch lightly in autumn and spring, at least until well established and give a light dressing of a balanced general fertilizer in spring. Leave to die down naturally after flowering. Leave undisturbed once established.

PROPAGATION

By division in spring or autumn.

PROBLEMS

None.

SITE Bog garden, full sun to light or almost moderate shade.
PREFERRED SOIL Preferably organic, acidic, low to moderate moisture.
HARDINESS Very hardy, tolerating -20°C (-4°F).
SIZE Will attain about 50 x 50cm (20 x 20in) after three or four years.

Molinia caerulea '**Variegata**'

GRASSES

Phalaris arundinacea 'Picta' Gardener's Garters

❝ *This is a very striking grass but think about it carefully before introducing it to your garden as it is most certainly one to plant with caution, for it is aggressively invasive. In saying that, it remains a plant that is seen very commonly in garden borders and I can only assume that it is planted by gardeners who have more time on their hands than I do, as it truly needs dividing and restraining annually. Its white and green striped leaves will look most appealing in the larger, wilder bog garden, however, where they can serve a very useful purpose in keeping weeds under control. I have even known couch grass take on gardener's garters and come away somewhat chastened.* ❞

CARE
Mulch in the autumn and spring until well established and give a light dressing of a balanced general fertilizer in the spring. Leave to die down naturally after flowering is completed. Remember to lift and divide the plant annually when it is being grown in anything that approaches a confined space.

PROPAGATION
By division in spring or autumn.

PROBLEMS
None.

RECOMMENDED VARIETIES
The variegated form is the only one recommended.

SITE Bog garden, full sun to light shade.
PREFERRED SOIL Tolerates almost any, low to moderate moisture.
HARDINESS Very hardy, tolerating -20°C (-4°F).
SIZE Will attain about 90 x 60cm (34 x 24in) within a year.

Schoenoplectus lacustris (syn. *Scirpus lacustris*)

❝ *One of the most widespread of aquatic rush species found in most of the northern hemisphere. It occurs in a good many gardens too, where its rather striking, variegated, round stems invariably arouse comment, although its leaves are more like those of a grass than a rush. One of the most effective uses I ever saw of this plant was of the banded-leaf form 'Zebrinus' in a complete interplanted mixture with the banded-stemmed form of the grass* Miscanthus sinensis, *also called 'Zebrinus' (p.114).* ❞

CARE
Mulch in autumn and spring, at least until well established, and give a balanced general fertilizer in spring. Leave to die down naturally after flowering. Leave undisturbed once fully established.

Schoenoplectus lacustris 'Zebrinus'

PROPAGATION
By division in spring or autumn.

PROBLEMS
None.

SITE Bog garden, full sun to light shade.
PREFERRED SOIL Tolerates most, low to moderate moisture.
HARDINESS Hardy, tolerating around -15°C (5°F).
SIZE Will attain a height of about 1m x 50cm (3ft x 20in) within three years.

RECOMMENDED VARIETIES
The normal species is quite commonly offered but has nothing special to recommend it. The two to choose are forms of the lower growing subspecies, *tabernaemontani*: 'Albescens', with white stems and longitudinal green stripes; 'Zebrinus', with green stems and the horizontal pale cream stripes.

Spartina pectinata 'Aureomarginata' Cord grass

 6 6 *Some species of* Spartina *are among the most important plants of the coastal salt marsh, where they tolerate periodic immersion, salt, wind and other environmental extremes. This should serve to indicate, first, that they might make good water garden plants, and second, that they are tough. Both facts are true and the variegated form I suggest not only has beautiful, dark green foliage with golden-edges, that turns a lovely gold all over in autumn, but also most appealing, slender flower stalks and inflorescences.* 9 9

SITE Bog garden, full sun to light shade.
PREFERRED SOIL Preferably not highly organic, moderate to high moisture.
HARDINESS Very hardy, tolerating -20°C (-4°F).
SIZE Will attain 1.5-1.8m x 75-90cm (5-6ft x 30-34in) within three years.

CARE
Mulch in autumn and spring, at least until well established and give a balanced general fertilizer in spring. Leave to die down naturally after flowering. Leave undisturbed once fully established.

PROPAGATION
By division in spring or autumn.

Spartina pectinata 'Aureomarginata'

PROBLEMS
None.

RECOMMENDED VARIETIES
The variegated form is the only one recommended.

Zizania aquatica Wild rice

 6 6 *'Wild rice?' You are probably echoing a gardening friend when I first told her the identity of one of my newest acquisitions. Yes, this is the North American plant that yields Indian or Tuscarora rice although it needs a warm climate to ripen. It is a true grass and the only annual one that I have included, but I do so as I have been asked about this plant so often recently that its seeds must now be generally available. It is an impressive species with soft foliage and dangling flowers but it needs a warm sheltered spot to give of its best.* 9 9

Zizania aquatica

SITE Marginal or water plant in shallow water.
PREFERRED SOIL Tolerates all types.
HARDINESS Barely hardy, tolerating -5°C (23°F).
SIZE Up to 3.5m x 60cm (12ft x 24in) in warm areas and so probably comes second only to the sunflower as the tallest-growing annual in a temperate climate.

CARE
None necessary once planted. Pull out at the end of the season.

PROPAGATION
From seed sown in spring in the greenhouse in pots of soil-based compost immersed in water. Plant out after the frosts. Note that the wild rice sold for human consumption may not germinate as it has often been heated to ripen it.

PROBLEMS
None.

RECOMMENDED VARIETIES
Normal species only is available.

BOG GARDEN TREES AND SHRUBS

Trees and shrubs are undoubtedly the plants least frequently used in water gardens. In many instances, this may well be because there is simply insufficient room; the average modern garden, after all, probably has room for only one or two trees in total. With shrubs, however, I rather suspect that it is due more to a lack of appreciation that water tolerant or even water-requiring species exist and are available. Yet trees, shrubs and water comprise a common enough mixture in the wild; think of tree-lined streamsides and the canopy that overhangs many a swamp and fen. Given a little additional thought and in some instances, admittedly, a little extra searching for nursery suppliers, a few small ornamental trees and shrubs can be found that would enhance many a water garden planting. I hope this brief selection will offer an incentive for you to be a little more adventurous therefore.

Alnus Alder

❝ *I am sure that the common* Alnus glutinosa *must be the most familiar riverside tree throughout the British Isles and although, in itself, the normal species is a thing of no great beauty, it does have more ornamental relatives suitable for larger water gardens. All will, indeed, make fairly substantial trees in due course, although those that I have selected are smaller than the native British plant. All alders are deciduous and the appeal lies principally in the colour and form of the leaves, although the catkins, too, are interesting, if not exactly pretty. It is the catkins, however, that reveal the generally unappreciated fact that alders are close relatives of the birches.* ❞

Alnus glutinosa

CARE

Mulch in autumn and spring until well established and give a balanced general fertilizer in spring. Stake for three or fours years after planting.

PROPAGATION

Not easy; the best forms don't come true from seed, but layering of most is generally successful if slow.

SITE Bog garden, full sun to moderate shade.
PREFERRED SOIL Tolerates almost any, low to high moisture.
HARDINESS Very hardy, tolerating -20°C (-4°F).
SIZE Will attain about 6 x 2m (20 x 6ft) after five to seven years, and approximately 12 x 5m (40 x 16ft) eventually.

PRUNING

None necessary.

RECOMMENDED VARIETIES

Alnus glutinosa 'Aurea', leaves yellow in spring, gradually turning green as summer progresses; 'Imperialis', superb, fresh green, deeply-divided, fern-like foliage; to my mind, the loveliest alder. *A. incana* 'Aurea', golden leaves, twigs and catkins in spring, then gradually turning green.

PROBLEMS

None.

Betula Birch

❝ Although closely related in the same family, Betulaceae, birches are not generally thought of as water-loving trees in the same way as alders. This is because they are less tolerant of very wet conditions, but also because they will grow in a wide range of soil types and the native British and European species seem less competitive in really wet sites and so are seen more often elsewhere. It's also important to choose birches carefully when intending to plant them in bog garden positions as some are much more appropriate and much less disease-prone than others. For all, however, it is the combination of small, fresh green leaves and attractive bark that is their special appeal. ❞

SITE Bog garden, full sun to moderate shade.
PREFERRED SOIL Tolerates almost any, low to high moisture.
HARDINESS Very hardy, tolerating -20°C (-4°F).
SIZE The tree-sized species will attain about 6 x 1.5m (20 x 5ft) after seven or eight years and about 14 x 5m (45 x 16ft) eventually. The shrubby species will slowly attain approximately 1.5m x 75cm (5ft x 30in).

RECOMMENDED VARIETIES

Betula nigra (river or black birch), soft green leaves, with bark that darkens to almost black with age. *B. papyrifera* (paper birch, canoe birch — the North American Indians used the bark to make canoes), large mid-green leaves, white, speckled bark, one of the most water tolerant of the white-barked birches. *B. glandulosa* and *B. nana* are two shrub-sized birch trees of Arctic or sub-Arctic regions with rather rounded leaves and erect, unusual but very attractive catkins.

PROPAGATION

From seed, sown in a mixture of sand and soil-based compost for stratifying (leave outdoors in terra-cotta seed pans over winter) and then placed in a cold-frame in spring.

PRUNING

None necessary and generally to be avoided because any open tissues on birches are likely to be invaded by wood-rotting fungi

PROBLEMS

Aphids, wood decay fungi.

Betula papyrifera

CARE

Mulch in the autumn and spring until well established and give a balanced general fertilizer in spring. Stake tree-sized species for about three or fours years after planting.

BOG GARDEN TREES AND SHRUBS

Metasequoia glyptostroboides
Dawn Redwood

❝ *Plant a* Metasequoia *and you plant a slice of history, but plant it wisely for it will become a very large tree. Its historical interest is immense. Ancient fossil specimens of the genus had been known for some time when, in 1941, living specimens of this species were found growing wild in China; truly a living fossil. Within a few years of its seed being taken to the West, it was being grown widely throughout the temperate region. It is one of the few deciduous conifers, with flattened, almost yew-like needles and shoots and rich, deeply-fissured, greyish-brown bark.* ❞

Metasequoia glyptostroboides

CARE
Mulch in autumn and spring until well established and give a balanced general fertilizer in spring. Stake for approximately three or fours years after planting.

PROPAGATION
From seed or from semi-hardwood cuttings in the summer, preferably rooted in a misting frame.

PRUNING
None necessary.

PROBLEMS
None.

RECOMMENDED VARIETIES
Normal species only is generally available although some upright growing forms (usually called 'Fastigiata' or 'National') are seen very occasionally.

SITE Bog garden, full sun to moderate shade.
PREFERRED SOIL Tolerates almost any, low to high moisture.
HARDINESS Very hardy, tolerating -20°C (-4°F).
SIZE Will attain about 7 x 2m (23 x 6ft) after five to seven years, and probably up to 20 x 5m (60 x 16ft) eventually.

Myrica
Bog myrtle

❝ *I have always loved myrtles, be they true* Myrtus *myrtles, or the unrelated* Myrica *myrtles. The water garden species, the appropriately named bog myrtle,* Myrica gale, *is a British native plant but not a well-known one outside its habitat of boggy areas on acidic moorlands. Those, indeed, are the conditions that it needs to succeed, but provide them and then plant it and you will be entranced by the golden catkins that appear in spring on leafless twigs and by the reddish-green, delightfully scented foliage that follows afterwards.* ❞

Myrica gale

SITE Bog garden, full sun to light shade.
PREFERRED SOIL Acidic, organic, moderate to high moisture content.
HARDINESS Very hardy, tolerating -20°C (-4°F).
SIZE Will attain approximately 1 x 1m (3 x 3ft) after three or four years and up to 2 x 2m (6 x 6ft) eventually.

CARE
Mulch in autumn and spring until well established and give a light dressing of bonemeal in the spring. Does not need staking.

PROPAGATION
From seed sown fresh into an acidic soilless compost, or from semi-hardwood cuttings in summer.

PRUNING
None necessary.

PROBLEMS
None.

RECOMMENDED VARIETIES
Normal species only is available.

Populus x candicans 'Aurora'

Populus Poplar

" Poplars need no introduction, for they are among the most familiar, large, deciduous, landscape trees; especially in wetter places. And buried in that sentence lie their two most important characteristics: they are large trees and most (although strangely not all), are very fond of water. To avoid the embarrassment of a plant larger than you expected, do choose carefully.

And to avoid the embarrassment of the roots forsaking the bog garden and heading for your drains, they should only be planted in large gardens, well away from buildings. For all varieties, it is the overall shape of the tree and the shape and colour of the foliage (sometimes with a characteristic balsam scent) that serve to make this the most appealing of trees. "

SITE Bog garden, full sun to light shade.
PREFERRED SOIL Tolerates most, moderate moisture (high moisture for *P. x candicans*).
HARDINESS Very hardy, tolerating -20°C (-4°F).
SIZE Varies (see Recommended Varieties) but don't be too put off by the potential ultimate height as they can be restrained by pruning.

CARE
Mulch in autumn and spring until well established and give a light dressing of a balanced general fertilizer in spring. Stake until the tree is four or five years old.

PROPAGATION
From hardwood cuttings taken in late autumn and struck in a sheltered position in the open garden.

PRUNING
None necessary but may be pruned hard in spring to limit the overall size, alter the shape or create a single, clear trunk.

RECOMMENDED VARIETIES
Most of the best garden poplars are hybrids of variable parentage, and among the most widely available are *Populus* x *canadensis* 'Aurea', golden-yellow leaves, gradually turning green, fast growing, eventually reaching up to 30m (100ft), can be rather spreading; *P.* x *candicans* 'Aurora', white and pink blotches on young green, scented leaves, fast growing to over 20m (60ft), but will respond well to pruning which encourages the attractive young foliage; *P. lasiocarpa*, very large, pale green leaves, slower growing than most poplars, eventually reaching a height of 8m (25ft) or more; *P. tremula* (aspen), very pretty leaves with whitish undersides which shimmer in the breeze, moderately fast-growing to reach 10m (30ft) or even more in some cases.

PROBLEMS
Aphids, rust, canker.

BOG GARDEN TREES AND SHRUBS

Salix Willow

❝ *One tree that has more of a reputation than the poplar for being water-loving must be its fellow genus in the same family,* Salix, *the willow. But oddly enough, while most poplars do have a fairly high requirement for water, the reputation of willows for charging into and along drain-pipes derives largely from the characteristics of only one species, the weeping willow, called for a* long time Salix babylonica, *then* S. x chrysocoma *and now, more accurately,* S. x sepulcralis *'Chrysocoma'. The weeping willow is, however, astonishingly lovely, with its fresh golden-green colour and its superbly pendulous and graceful form. If you have a really large garden and a water garden to match at a distance from your house, then don't deny yourself this plant.* ❞

CARE
Mulch in autumn and spring until well established and give a balanced general fertilizer in spring. Stake for approximately three or four years after planting.

PROPAGATION
From hardwood cuttings in late autumn; nothing will strike more easily. Push them into any except the very driest soil and they will root with consummate ease.

PRUNING
None necessary, but almost all the willows may be pruned hard in spring to limit size or to correct shape. The large, tree-sized willows may be routinely pollarded, although this should not be done with the weeping willow which, as a result, would weep no more. The exceptionally striking, coloured-stemmed varieties of *S. alba* and *S. daphnoides* are best pollarded, however, to encourage the attractive young growth.

PROBLEMS
Aphids, anthracnose die-back on weeping willows.

Salix alba vitellina 'Britzensis'

SITE Bog garden, full sun to light shade.
PREFERRED SOIL Tolerates almost any, low to high moisture.
HARDINESS Very hardy, tolerating -20°C (-4°F).
SIZE Varies with species and variety (see Recommended Varieties); the species that I recommend pruning to enhance their coloured bark should attain a height of up to about 2m (6ft) each year.

RECOMMENDED VARIETIES
The normal hybrid weeping willow will be the only form seen of this plant, but other good willows for the bog garden are: *Salix caprea* 'Pendula' (Kilmarnock willow), small weeping head with pretty spring catkins, usually grafted onto a rootstock 2-3m (6-10ft) in height; *S. purpurea* 'Pendula', small. weeping tree to about 3-4m (10-13ft) with narrow, purple-green leaves; *S. alba vitellina* 'Britzensis' (also called 'Chermesina'), orange-red winter bark colour; *S. a. sericea* (also called *argentea*), silver willow, silvery-grey leaves, very striking; *S. daphnoides*, purplish shoots with white powdery bloom.

Taxodium distichum Swamp cypress

❝ *Surely, a plant called the swamp cypress must be* the conifer for a bog garden. Yes, it certainly grows naturally by the creeks and swamps of the southern United States but, in Britain, it seems to find a good, deep, rich soil and a fairly mild climate more important than having its roots in water. Like that other bog garden tree,* Metasequoia, *it is one of those rarities, a deciduous conifer and it, too, has rather flattened, almost feathery shoots. It is also a large tree but, given the space, it makes a fine and noble plant.* ❞

SITE Bog garden, full sun to light or moderate shade.
PREFERRED SOIL Rich, deep, low to high moisture.
HARDINESS Hardy, tolerating about -15°C (5°F).
SIZE Will attain approximately 5 x 1.5m (16 x 5ft) after five years and up to 30m (100ft) in height eventually.

Taxodium distichum

CARE

Mulch in autumn and spring until well established and give a balanced general fertilizer in spring. Stake for approximately three or four years after planting.

PROPAGATION

By seed, sown in a humus-enriched, soil-based compost in a sheltered cold-frame or in a propagator in the spring.

PRUNING

None necessary.

PROBLEMS

None.

RECOMMENDED VARIETIES

The normal species will be the only one seen.

Vaccinium

" *Vaccinium is a valuable genus that needs no real introduction to someone with acid soil, but is of little interest to anyone who doesn't have it. It embraces a large number of species grown for their fruit (blueberries, cranberries and huckleberries among others) as well as foliage shrubs and ground cover species. Most tolerate, if not require, wet conditions and while some are undeniably dull, there are others that make excellent subjects for the acidic bog garden.* "

SITE Bog garden, full sun to light shade.
PREFERRED SOIL Organic, acidic, low to moderate moisture.
HARDINESS Hardy to very hardy, tolerating -15 to -20°C (5 to -4°F) unless stated otherwise.
SIZE Varies (see Recommended Varieties).

CARE

Mulch in autumn and spring with acidic compost, such as chopped conifer needles or sawdust, and give a balanced general fertilizer in spring.

PROPAGATION

By semi-ripe cuttings in spring or hardwood cuttings in late autumn, put in an acidic, soilless compost in a cold-frame.

PRUNING

None necessary.

PROBLEMS

None.

RECOMMENDED VARIETIES

Among almost 500 species, the following are widely available, attractive and small enough to plant in a modestly sized bog garden. I have described others in Books 2 and 4 of this series (*Best Foliage Shrubs* and *Best Soft Fruit*).

Vaccinium vitis-idaea (cowberry), evergreen, slow-growing, creeping, up to 30cm (12in) tall, white flowers with pink tinge in late summer, edible red fruits. There are a number of named selections but these have been selected principally on the basis of their fruiting quality. *V. delavayi*, evergreen, neat shrub up to 30 x 20cm (12 x 18in), small clusters of cream-white flowers in late summer, red-purple fruits. *V. glaucoalbum*, evergreen, compact shrub of dense habit, up to 1m x 45cm (3ft x 18in), white flowers in early summer, black fruit; attractive but only fairly hardy, tolerating -5 to -10°C (23-14°F). *V. nummularia*, evergreen, many branched shrub, up to about 45 x 25cm (18 x 12in), very pretty pink flowers in spring, edible black fruits.

Vaccinium vitis-idaea

INDEX

Page numbers in *italic*
refer to illustrations

Acorus
A. *calamus* 22, *22*
A. *gramineus* 22
A. g. 'Variegatus' 22
Ajuga
A. *pyramidalis* 67
A. *reptans* 67, *67*
A. r. 'Alba' 67
A. r. 'Atropurpurea' 67
A. r. 'Burgundy Glow'
67
A. r. 'Multicolor' 67
A. r. 'Rainbow' 67
A. r. 'Variegata' 67
Alchemilla
A. *alpina* 66
A. *conjuncta* 66
A. *mollis* 66, *66*
Alder see *Alnus*
algae 20-1
Alisma
A. *lanceolatum* 23
A. *parviflorum* 23
A. *plantago-aquatica* 22-3,
23
Alnus 118
A. *glutinosa* *118*
A. *glutinosa* 'Aurea' 118
A. g. 'Imperialis' 118
A. *incana* 'Aurea' 118
Alopecurus pratensis
'Aureovariegatus'
106, *106*
A. *p.* 'Aureus' 106
Amphibious bistort see
Polygonum
amphibium
Anaphilis margaritacea 66,
67
A. m. *cinnamomea* 66
A. m. 'Neuschnee' 66
Aponogeton distachyos 38,
38
Arrow arum see *Peltandra*
undulata
Artimisia lactiflora 68, *68*
Arum italicum 69
A. *i.* 'Pictum' 69, *69*
Aruncus
A. *dioicus* 68-9, *69*
A. 'Kneiffii' 68, *69*
Aspen see *Populus*
tremula
Astilbe hybrids 70, *70*
A. 'Snowdrift' 70
Azolla
A. *caroliniana* 60, *60*
A. *filiculoides* 60

baskets, planting 16
Bergenia 70-1
B. *cordifolia* 'Bressingham
Ruby' 71
B. c. 'Bressingham
White' 71
B. c. 'Purpurea' 71, *71*
Betula 119
B. *glandulosa* 119
B. *nana* 119
B. *nigra* 119
B. *papyrifera* 119, *119*
Birch see *Betula*
Bladderwort see
Utricularia vulgaris
blanket weed 20-1
Bleeding heart see
Dicentra formosa
Bog arum see *Calla*
palustris
Bog bean see *Menyanthes*
trifoliata
bog gardens 9, 14-15
building 11-12
plants 14-15, 16, 66-101,
118-23
Bog myrtle see *Myrica*
Brass buttons see *Cotula*
coronopifolia
Broad buckler fern see
Dryopteris dilatata
Brunnera macrophylla 71,
71
B. m. 'Dawson's White'
71
B. m. 'Hadspen Cream'
71
B. m. 'Langtrees' 71
Bugle see *Ajuga reptans*
Burr reed see *Sparganium*
erectum
Butomus umbellatus 23, *23*

Calla lily see *Zantedeschia*
aethiopica
Calla palustris 24, *24*
Callitriche 52
C. *hermaphroditica* (syn.
autumnalis) 52
C. *palustris* 52, *52*
C. *verna* 52
Caltha
C. *leptostyla* 25
C. *palustris* 24, 25, *33*
C. p. 'Alba' 24
C. p. 'Flore Pleno' 24, *25*
Campanula lactiflora 72
C. *l.* 'Alba' 72, *72*
C. *l.* 'Loddon Anna' 72
C. *l.* 'Pritchard's Fancy'
72

Canadian pondweed see
Elodea canadensis
Cape pondweed see
Aponogeton
distachyos
Carex
C. *elata* 'Bowles' Golden'
107
C. *e.* 'Aurea' 107, *107*
C. *morrowii* 'Variegata'
107
C. *pseudocyperus* 107
C. *sylvatica* 107
Catchfly see *Lychnis*
chalcedonica
Ceratophyllum demersum
52-3, *53*
Cimicifuga 72-3
C. *racemosa* 73, *73*
C. *r.* 'Purpurea' 73
C. *simplex*
'Atropurpurea' 73
Common duckweed see
Lemna minor
Cord grass see *Spartina*
pectinata
Corkscrew rush see
Juncus effusus
'Spiralus'
Cortaderia selloana 108,
108
C. *s.* 'Aureolineata' 108
C. *s.* 'Golden Band' 108
C. *s.* 'Pumila' 108
C. *s.* 'Sunningdale Silver'
108
Cotton grass see
Eriophorum
angustifolium
Cotula coronopifolia 25, *25*
Cowberry see *Vaccinium*
vitis-idaea
Crassula helmsii (syn.
Tillaea recurva) 53,
53
Cream buttons see *Cotula*
coronopifolia
Creeping soft grass see
Holcus mollis
Cyperus sedges 108, *109*
C. *alternifolius* 108
C. *eragrostis* 108, *109*
C. *involucratus* 108, *109*
C. *longus* 108, 109

Dawn redwood see
Metasequoia
glyptostroboides
Day lily see *Hemerocallis*
Dicentra
D. *formosa* 73

D. *f.* 'Alba' 73, *73*
D. 'Pearl Drops' 73
D. *spectablis* 'Alba' 73
Dodecatheon 74
D. *dentatum* 74
D. *hendersonii* 74
D. *meadia* 74, *74*
D. *pulchellum* 74
D. *p.* 'Red Wings' 74
Dryopteris
D. *carthusiana* 102
D. *dilatata* 102, *103*
D. *d.* 'Crispa
Whiteside' 102
D. *d.* 'Lepidota Cristata'
102
D. *wallichiana* 102
Duckweed see *Lemna*

Egeria densa see *Elodea*
densa
Eichhornia crassipes 60-1,
61
Eleocharis
E. *acicularis* 54, *54*, 109,
109
E. *palustris* 109
Elephant's ears see
Bergenia
Elodea canadensis 54-5, *54*
E. *collitrichoides* 54
E. *crispa* 54
E. *densa* 54
E. *nuttallii* 54
Equisetum hyemale 26, *26*
Eriophorum angustifolium
110, *110*
Eupatorium 74-5
E. *cannabinum* 74, *75*
E. *c.* 'Flore Pleno' 75
E. *maculatum* 75
E. *m.* 'Atropurpureum'
75
Euphorbia palustris 75, *75*

Fairy moss see *Azolla*
caroliniana
ferns 102-5
fertilizer 16, 21
Filipendula
F. *palmata* 76
F. *purpurea* 76
F. *rubra* 76
F. *ulmaria* 'Flore Pleno'
76
F. *u.* 'Aurea' 76, *76*
F. *u.* 'Rosea' 76
filters 21
fish 18-19
Floating heart see
Nymphoides peltata

floating plants 14, 60-5
Flowering rush see
Butomus umbellatus
Foam flower see *Tiarella*
cordifolia
Fontinalis antipyretica 55,
55
fountains 8-9
Fringed water lily see
Nymphoides peltata
Fritillaria meleagris 76, *77*
F. m. *alba* 76
Frogbit see *Hydrocharis*
morsus-ranae
frogs 19

Gentian see *Gentiana*
Gentiana 77
G. *asclepiadea* 77
G. *a.* alba 77
G. *pneumonanthe* 77, *77*
Geranium phaeum 78, *78*
G. *p.* 'Album' 78
Geum rivale 78-9
G. *r.* 'Leonard's Variety'
78, *78*
G. *r.* 'Lionel Cox' 78
Globe flower see *Trollius*
Glyceria maxima
'Variegata' 110-11,
111
Goat's beard see *Aruncus*
dioicus
Golden club see *Orontium*
aquaticum
grasses 106-17
Gunnera
G. *manicata* 79, *79*
G. *tinctoria* 79

Hakonechloa
H. 'Alboaurea' 111, *111*
H. 'Aureola' 111
H. *macra* 111, *111*
Helioniopsis orientalis 80,
80
Hemerocallis 80-1
H. 'Anzac' 81
H. 'Black Magic' 81
H. 'Burning Daylight' 81
H. 'Catherine
Woodbery' 81
H. 'Hyperion' 81
H. 'Pink Damask' *80*
H. 'Stella de Oro' 81
Himalayan cowslip see
Primula florindae
Hippuris vulgaris 38-9, *39*
Holcus mollis
'Albovariegatus' 112,
112

Hornwort see
    Ceratophyllum
    demersum
Hosta 81
    H. 'Blue Moon' 81
    H. decorata 81
    H. fortunei 81
      H. f. albopicta 81
    H. 'Francee' 81
    H. 'Gingko Craig' 81
    H. lancifolia 81
    H. 'Thomas Hogg' 81
    H. undulata marginata 81,
     81
Hottonia palustris 61, *61*
Houttuynia cordata 26, *27*
    H. c. 'Chameleon' 26, *27*
    H. c. 'Flore Pleno' *27*
Hydrocharis morsus-ranae
    62, *62*
Hypericum elodes 27, *27*

insect life 19
Iris
    I. 'Caesar's Brother' 83
    I. chrysographes 82, *82,*
     83
     I. c. 'Black Knight' 83
    I. 'Ego' 83
    I. ensata (syn.
     I. kaempferi) 28, *28*
    I. e. 'Alba' 28
    I. e. 'Higo' hybrids 28
    I. e. 'Moonlight Waves'
     28
    I. e. 'Rose Queen' 28
    I. e. 'Variegata' 28
    I. 'Helen Astor' 83
    I. innominata 82, *83*
    I. laevigata 28
     I. l. 'Alba' 28
     I. l. 'Atro-purpurea' 28
     I. l. 'Colchesterensis' 28
     I. l. 'Midnight' 28
     I. l. 'Variegata' 28, *29*
    I. 'Mrs Rowe' 83
    I. orientalis 82, *83*
    I. 'Papillon' 83
    I. pseudocorus 28, *29*
     I. p. 'Alba' 28
     I. p. bastardii 28
     I. p. 'Variegata' 28
    I. sanguinea 83
    I. sibirica 82, *82, 83*
    I. 'Sparkling Rose' 83
    I. 'Tropic Night' 83
    I. versicolor 28
     I. v. 'Kermesina' 28
     I. v. 'Wisley White' 83
Ivy-leaved duckweed see
    Lemna trisulca

Japanese rush see *Acorus*
    gramineus
Juncus effusus 'Spiralus'
    112, *113*

Kaffir lily see *Schizostylis*
    coccinea
Kilmarnock willow see
    Salix caprea
Kingcup see *Caltha*
    palustris

Lady's mantle see
    Alchemilla mollis
Lemna
    L. gibba 63, *63*
    L. minor 63
    L. polyrhiza 63
    L. trisulca 63
Leucojum 83
    L. aestivum 83, *83*
    L. vernumis 83
Lizard's tail see *Saururus*
    cernuus
Lobelia
    L. cardinalis 29, *29*
    L. dortmanna 29, 56, *56*
    L. fulgens 29
    L. 'Queen Victoria' 29
Logarosiphon major see
    Elodea crispa
Lungwort see *Pulmonaria*
Luzula 113, *113*
    L. maxima 113
    L. nivea 113
    L. sylvatica 113
     L. s. 'Aurea' 113
     L. s. 'Marginata' 113
Lychnis
    L. chalcedonica 84, *84*
     L. c. 'Alba' 84
     L. c. 'Flore Pleno' 84
    L. flos-cuculi 84
    L. x haogeana 84
Lysichiton 84-5
    L. americanus 85
    L. camtschatcense 85, *85*
Lysimachia
    L. nemorum 85
    L. nummularia 'Aurea' 85,
     85
    L. punctata 85
Lythrum
    L. 'Firecandle' 86
    L. 'Robert' 86
    L. salicaria 86, *86*
    L. virgatum 86
     L. v. 'Rosy Gem' 86
     L. v. 'The Rocket' 86

Mare's tail see *Hippuris*

    vulgaris
marginals 14, 16, 22-37
Marliac, Joseph Bory
    Latour 47
Marsh cinqufoil see
    Potentilla palustris
Marsh fern see *Thelypteris*
    palustris
Marsh Marigold see *Caltha*
    palustris
Marsh St. John's Wort see
    Hypericum elodes
Matteuccia struthiopteris
    103, *103*
Meadow foxtail grass see
    Alopecurus pratensis
Meadowsweet see
    Filipendula
Mentha aquatica 30, *30*
Menyanthes trifoliata 30-1
Merry bells see *Uvularia*
Metasequoia
    glyptostroboides 120,
     120
    M. g. 'Fasigiata' 120
    M. g. 'National' 120
Milium effusum 'Aureum'
    114, *114*
Mimulus 31, *31*
    M. x bartonianus 31
    M. lewisii 31
    M. luteus 31, *31*
    M. moschatus 31
    M. ringens 31
Miscanthus sinensis 114-15,
    115
    M. s. 'Gracillimus' 115
    M. s. 'Silberfeder' 115
    M. s. 'Variegatus' 115
    M. s. 'Zebrinus' 115, 116
Molinia caerulea 115, *115*
    M. c. 'Variegata' 115
Moor grass see *Molinia*
    caerulea
mulching 16
Musk see *Mimulus*
Myosotis scorpioides 32, *32,*
    36
    M. s. 'Mermaid' 32
    M. s. 'Pinkie' 32
Myrica 120-1, *120*
Myriophyllum 56-7, *57*
    M. aquaticum 56, *57*
    M. spicatum 56, *57*
    M. verticillatum 56, *57, 57*

Needle spike rush see
    Eleocharis acicularis
New Zealand flax see
    Phormium
newts 19

Nile grass see *Cyperus*
    involucratus
Nuphar
    N. japonica 40
    N. lutea 40, *40*
    N. pumila 40
    N. variegata 40
Nymphaea 42-7, *42, 43,*
    46, 47
    N. alba 43, 45
    N. 'Albatross' 46
    N. 'Amabilis' *43*, 45
    N. 'Atropurpurea' 45
    N. 'Attraction' 45
    N. 'Aurora' 46
    N. 'Brackleyi Rosea' 46
    N. 'Caroliniana Nivea' 45
    N. 'Charles de Meurville'
     45
    N. 'Colonel A. J. Welch'
     45
    N. 'Colossea' *43*, 45
    N. 'Commanche' 46
    N. 'Conqueror' 45, *47*
    N. 'Ellisiana' 46
    N. 'Escarboucle' 45
    N. 'Firecrest' 46
    N. 'Froebelii' 46, *46*
    N. 'Gladstoniana' 45
    N. 'Gloire du Temple-
     sur-Lot' 45
    N. 'Gloriosa' 46
    N. 'Gonnäre' *43*, 45
    N. 'Graziella' 46
    N. x helvola 46, *46*
    N. 'Indiana' 46
    N. 'James Brydon' 46, *46*
    N. 'Laydekeri Fulgens' 46
    N. 'Laydekeri Lilacea' 46
    N. 'Laydekeri Purpurata'
     46
    N. 'Madame Wilfron
     Gonnäre' *42*, 45
    N. 'Marliacea Albida' 45
    N. 'Marliacea Carnea' 45
    N. 'Marliacea
     Chromatella' *43*, 45
    N. 'Marliacea Rosea' 45
    N. 'Masaniello' *43*, 45
    N. 'Moorei' *43*, 45
    N. 'Mrs. Richmond' *43*,
     45
    N. odorata 45
    N. 'Odorata Sulphurea
     Grandiflora' 46
    N. 'Odorata William B.
     Shaw' 45
    N. 'Paul Hariot' 46
    N. 'René Gerard' *44*, 45
    N. 'Robinsoniana' 46
    N. 'Rose Arey' 46

    N. 'Sioux' 46
    N. 'Solfatare' 46
    N. 'Sunrise' 45
    N. tetrogona (syn.
     'Pygmaea Alba') 46
    N. tuberosa 'Richardsonii'
     45
    N. t. 'Rosea' 45
    N. 'William Falconer' 45
Nymphoides peltata 41, *41*
    N. p. 'Bennettii' 41

Obedient plant see
    Physostegia virginiana
Onoclea sensiblis 104, *104*
Ornamental rhubarb see
    Rheum
Orontium aquaticum 48, *48*
Osmunda regalis 104-5,
    105
    O. r. purpurascens 105

Pampas grass see
    Cortaderia selloana
Parochetus communis 86,
    87
Pearly everlasting see
    Anaphilis
    margaritacea
Peltandra undulata (syn.
    virginica) 32-3, *33*
Peltiphyllum peltatum (syn.
    Darmera peltata) 87,
    87
    P. p. 'Nana' 87
Persicaria
    P. amplexicaulis 89, *89*
     P. a. 'Arun Gem' 89
     P. a. 'Atrosanguinea' 89
     P. a. pendula 89
    P. campanulata 89
     P. c. 'Alba' 89
    P. millettii 89
pests and diseases 20-1
Phalaris arundinacea 'Picta'
    116, *116*
Phormium
    P. cookianum 'Maori' 88
     P. c. 'Sundowner' 88
    P. 'Rainbow Surprise' *88,*
     89
    P. tenax 88
     P. t. 'Nanum
      Purpureum' 88
     P. t. 'Purpureum' 88
Physostegia virginiana 88-9,
    89
    P. v. 'Alba' 89
    P. v. 'Bouquet Rose' 89
    P. v. 'Crown of Snow' 89
    P. v. 'Summer Snow' 89

INDEX

P. v. 'Vivid' 89
Pickerel weed see
    Pontederia cordata
Plantain lily see *Hosta*
Polecat weed see
    Symplocarpus foetidus
Polygonum amphibium (syn.
    Persicaria amphibia)
    49, *49*
Pond lily see *Nuphar*
Pondweed see
    Potamogeton
Pontederia
  P. alba 50
  P. azurea see *Eichornia*
    crassipes
  P. cordata 50, *50*
  P. lanceolata 50
pools
  building 10-11
  formal and informal 8
  raised 12
  siting 9
Poplar see *Populus*
Populus 121
  P. x canadensis 'Aurea'
    121, *121*
  P. x c. 'Aurora' 121
  P. lasiocarpa 121
  P. tremula 121
Potamogeton 58
  P. crispus 58
  P. pectinatus 58, *58*
Potentilla palustris 90, *90*
Primula 90-1
  P. alpicola 91
  P. anisodora 91
  P. beesiana 91
  P. x bulleesiana 91
  P. bulleyana 91
  P. burmanica 91
  P. chungensis 91
  P. cockburniana 91
  P. denticulata 91
  P. d. alba 91
  P. d. 'Inshriach
    Carmine' 91
  P. florindae 91, *91*
  P. helodoxa 91
  P. Inshriach Hybrids 91
  P. 'Inverewe' 91
  P. japonica 91
  P. j. 'Miller's Crimson'
    91
  P. j. 'Postford White'
    91
  P. pulverulenta 90, *90*, 91,
    91
  P. rosea 91
  P. r. 'Grandiflora' 91
propagation 16

Pulmonaria 92
  P. angustifolia 'Munstead
    Blue' 92
  P. longifolia 'Bertram
    Anderson' 92
  P. 'Mawson's Blue' 92
  P. officinalis 92
  P. o. 'Sissinghurst
    White' 92

Ranunculus 33, *33*
  R. aquatilis 33, 59, *59*
  R. flammula 33
  R. lingua 33, *33*
  R. l. 'Grandiflorus' 33
Reedmace see *Typha*
Rheum 92-3
  R. 'Ace of Hearts' 93
  R. pulmatum 93
  R. p. 'Atrosanguineum'
    92, *93*
  R. p. rubrum 93
Rodgersia 93
  R. aesculifolia 93, *93*
  R. pinnata 93
  R. p. 'Elegans' 93
  R. p. 'Superba' 93
  R. podophylla 93
  R. sambucifolia 93
Royal fern see *Osmunda
    regalis*

Sagittaria
  S. japonica 34
  S. sagittifolia 34, *34*
  S. s. 'Flore Pleno' 34
Salix 122
  S. alba sericea 122
  S. a. vitellina 'Britzensis'
    122
  S. a. v. 'Chermesina'
    122, *122*
  S. caprea 'Pendula' 122
  S. daphnoides 122
  S. purpurea 'Pendula' 122
  S. x sepulcralis
    'Chrysoscoma' 122
Saururus cernuus 94, *94*
Saxifraga fortunei 94-5, *95*
  S. f. 'Rubrifolia' 95
  S. f. 'Wada' 95
Schizostylis coccinea 95
  S. c. alba 95
  S. c. 'Jennifer' 95
  S. c. 'Major' 95
  S. c. 'Mrs Hegarty' 95
  S. c. 'Professor Barnard' 95
  S. c. 'Vicountess Byng'
    95, *95*
Schoenoplectus
  S. lacustris (syn. *Scirpus*

    lacustris) 116
  S. l. 'Zebrinus' *116*
  S. tabernaemontani
    'Zebrinus' 116
  S. t. 'Albescens' 116
Scouring rush see
    Equisetum hyemale
Sensitive fern see *Onoclea
    sensiblis*
Shooting stars see
    Dodecatheon
shrubs 118-23
Shuttlecock fern see
    *Matteuccia
    struthiopteris*
Skunk cabbage see
    Lysichiton
snails 19
Snakeshead see *Fritillaria
    meleagris*
Snowflake see *Leucojum*
Snowy woodrush see
    Luzula nivea
Sparganium erectum 51, *51*
Spartina pectinata
    'Aureomarginata'
    117, *117*
Spearwort see *Ranunculus*
Spiderwort see
    *Tradescantia
    virginiana*
Spike rush see *Eleocharis
    acicularis*
Stratiotes aloides 64, *64*
Stylophorum
  S. diphyllum 96, *96*
  S. lasiocarpum 96
submerged plants 14, 16,
    52-9
Swamp cypress see
    Taxodium distichum
Swamp lily see *Saururus
    cernuus*
Sweet flag see *Acorus
    calamus*
Symplocarpus foetidus 96-
    7, *96*

Taxodium distichum 122-3,
    123
Thalictrum
  T. flavum 97, *97*
  T. f. glaucum 97
  T. f. 'Illuminator' 97
Thelypteris palustris 105, *105*
Tiarella
  T. collina 98
  T. cordifolia 98, *98*
  T. polyphylla 98
  T. wherryi 98
Toad lily see *Tricyrtis hirta*

Tradescantia
  T. x andersoniana
    'Innocence' 99
  T. x a. 'Isis' 99
  T. x a. 'Osprey' 99
  T. x a. 'Purple Dome'
    99
  T. x a. 'Zwanenburg
    Blue' 99
  T. virginiana 98-9, *99*
Trapa natans 64-5, *65*
trees 118-23
Tricyrtis
  T. formosana 99
  T. hirta 99
  T. h. alba 99
  T. h. 'Miyazaki' 99
  T. h. 'Variegata' 99
  T. latifolia 99, *99*
Trollius
  T. chinensis 'Golden
    Queen' 100
  T. x cultorum 'Earliest of
    All' 100
  T. x c. 'Feuertroll' 100
  T. x c. 'Golden Queen'
    100
  T. x c. 'Goldquelle' 100
  T. x c. 'Orange
    Princess' 100
  T. europaeus 100, *100*
  T. pumilus 100
tub garden 8
Tufted sedge see *Carex
    elata* 'Aurea'
Typha 34-5
  T. angustifolia 35, *35*
  T. latifolia 35, *35*
  T. laxmannii 35
  T. minima 34, 35, *35*

Umbrella plant see
    *Cyperus involucratus;
    Peltiphyllum
    peltatum*
Utricularia vulgaris 65, *65*
Uvularia 100
  U. grandiflora 100, *101*

Vaccinium 123
  V. delavayi 123
  V. glaucoalbum 123
  V. nummularia 123
  V. vitis-idaea 123, *123*
Veratrum 101
  V. nigrum 101, *101*
Veronica beccabunga 36, *36*
Water Avens see *Geum
    rivale*
Water chestnut see *Trapa
    natans*

Water crowfoot see
    Ranunculus aquatilis
Water forget-me-not see
    Myosotis scorpioides
water gardens
  creating 10
  as feature 8-9
Water Hawthorn see
    *Aponogeton
    distachyos*
Water hyacinth see
    Eichornia crassipes
Water irises see *Iris*
Water lily see *Nuphar;
    Nymphaea*
Water lobelia see *Lobelia
    dortmanna*
Water milfoil see
    Myriophyllum
Water mint see *Mentha
    aquatica*
Water moss see *Fontinalis
    antipyretica*
water movement and
    lighting 12-13
Water plantain see *Alisma
    plantago-aquatica*
water plants 14, 16, 38-51
Water soldier see
    Stratiotes aloides
Water starwort see
    Callitriche
Water violet see *Hottonia
    palustris*
Weeping willow see *Salix
    x sepulcralis
    'Chrysoscoma'*
Wild rice see *Zizania
    aquatica*
Willow grass see
    *Polygonum
    amphibium*
Willow moss see
    Fontinalis antipyretica
Willow see *Salix*
Wood millett see *Milium
    effusum*
Wood poppy see
    *Stylophorum
    diphyllum*
Wood sedge see *Carex
    sylvatica*
Woodrush see *Luzula*

Zantedeschia aethiopica
    36-7, *37*
  Z. a. 'Crowborough' 37
  Z. a. 'Green Goddess'
    37, *37*
Zizania aquatica 117, *117*

PHOTOGRAPHIC ACKNOWLEDGEMENTS

Front cover: Photos Horticultural **Back cover:** Professor Stefan Buczacki

Inside photographs:

James Allison 25, 40 right; Heather Angel 96 left; Aquila Photographics /J Mathieson 10, 11, 12, 13, /R J Orr 78 top; A-Z Botanical Collection /Michael R Chandler 101 bottom, /Anthony Cooper 84, /Bjorn Svensson 26; Gillian Beckett 105 bottom, 114, 122; Pat Brindley 35 left, 39, 116; Bruce Coleman Ltd 117 right, /Eric Crichton 69 top, /Andy Purcell 19, /Hans Reinhard 65 top; Eric Crichton 6, 15, 23 right, 29 right, 33 bottom, 43 centre right, 43 centre, 68, 82 top, 82 bottom, 83, 85 bottom, 89 right, 93, 107, 112, 115 right; John Fielding 25 top, 53 centre, 57 top, 67 left, 72, 87 left, 96 right; Garden Picture Library/David England 57 bottom; John Glover 7, 9, 29 top left, 48, 71 bottom, 77 top, 85 top, 88, 90 right, 92 left, 105 top, 109 left, 111 bottom; Andrew Lawson 23 left, 32, 42, 43 bottom left, 43 bottom right, 46 centre, 46 left, 47, 60, 67 right, 69 bottom, 73 left, 74 left, 75, 78 bottom, 87 right, 89 left, 91, 106, 117 left, 120 right, 121, 123 bottom; Natural Image /Robin Fletcher 123 left, /Bob Gibbons 30, 38, 55, 56, 58, 61 left, 65 bottom, 90 left, /Peter Wilson 120 left; Nature Photographers Ltd /Brinsley Burbidge 99 right, /Jean Hall 22, 64, /LG Jessup 34, /David Rae 25 bottom, /Paul Sterry 53 top right, 74 right, /Roger Tidman 40 bottom, /Andrew Weston 100; Clive Nichols 103 right; Oxford Scientific Films /Deni Bown 95 top; Photos Horticultural 1, 8, 14, 20, 36, 37 top, 37 bottom, 43 top right, 43 top left, 44, 46 right, 53 top left, 54 bottom, 70, 71 top, 73 right, 76, 77 bottom, 79, 80 top, 80 bottom, 92 right, 108, 111 top left, 113 bottom, 113 top, 119; Premaphotos Wildlife / K G Preston-Mafham 41, 62, 63, 103 left, 118; Reed Consumer Books Picture Library 115 top, /Jerry Harpur 29 bottom right, 81, 104, 111 top right; Harry Smith Collection 16, 18, 21, 27 top, 27 bottom, 28, 31, 33 top, 35 right, 35 centre, 43 centre left, 43 top centre, 43 bottom centre, 49, 50, 51, 52, 54 top, 59, 66, 86, 95 bottom, 97, 98, 99 left, 101 top, 109 right, 110; Stapley Water Gardens 94; Elizabeth Whiting & Associates 61 right.

TEMPERATURE CHART

BARELY HARDY	0 to -5°C	32 to 23°F
FAIRLY HARDY	-5 to -10°C	23 to 14°F
MODERATELY HARDY	-10 to -15°C	14 to 5°F
HARDY	-15 to -20°C	5 to -4°F
VERY HARDY	-20°C or below	-4°F or below

STEFAN BUCZACKI "BEST" SERIES J502D60C

The complete range is available from all good bookshops or by Mail Order direct from the publisher. Payment can be made by credit card or cheque/postal order in the following ways:

BY PHONE Phone through your order on our special CREDIT CARD HOTLINE on **0933 410511**. Speak to our customer service team during office hours (9am to 5pm) or leave a message on the answer machine, quoting your full credit card number plus expiry date and your full name and address. Please also quote the reference number shown at the top of this form.

BY POST Simply fill out the order form below (it can be photocopied) and send it with your payment to:

REED BOOK SERVICES LTD, PO BOX 5, RUSHDEN, NORTHANTS NN10 6YX.

SPECIAL OFFER: FREE POSTAGE AND PACKAGING FOR ALL ORDERS OVER £10, add £2.00 for p+p if your order is for £10 or less.

ISBN	TITLE	PRICE	QUANTITY	TOTAL
0 600 57732 5	Best Climbers	4.99		
0 600 57735 X	Best Foliage Shrubs	4.99		
0 600 57734 1	Best Shade Plants	4.99		
0 600 57733 3	Best Soft Fruit	4.99		
0 600 58337 6	Best Water Plants	4.99		
0 600 58338 4	Best Herbs	4.99		
		Postage & Packaging (add £2 for p+p if your order is £10 or less)		
		GRAND TOTAL		

Name .... (BLOCK CAPITALS)

Address ....

.... Postcode ....

I enclose a cheque/postal order for £ .... made payable to Reed Book Services Ltd or

Please debit my: Access ☐ Visa ☐ AmEx account ☐ Diners ☐ by £ .... Expiry date ....

Account no ☐☐☐☐☐☐☐☐☐☐☐☐☐☐☐☐ Signature ....

Whilst every effort is made to keep our prices low, the publisher reserves the right to increase the prices at short notice.
Your order will be dispatched within 28 days subject to availability.
Registered office: Michelin House, 81 Fulham Road, London SW3 6RB. Registered in England no 1974080

THIS FORM MAY BE PHOTOCOPIED